Soul Satisfaction

Also by Debra Evans

The Complete Book on Childbirth
The Mystery of Womanhood
Heart and Home
Fragrant Offerings
Beauty for Ashes
Without Moral Limits
Blessed Events
Preparing for Childbirth
The Woman's Complete Guide to Personal Health Care
Beauty and the Best
Christian Parenting Answers (General Editor)
Women of Character
Kindred Hearts
Ready or Not, You're a Grandparent
The Christian Woman's Guide to Sexuality
The Christian Woman's Guide to Personal Health Care
Women of Courage
The Christian Woman's Guide to Childbirth
Without Moral Limits (Revised Edition)

SOUL SATISFACTION

For Women Who Long for More

DEBRA EVANS

CROSSWAY BOOKS • WHEATON, ILLINOIS
A DIVISION OF GOOD NEWS PUBLISHERS

Soul Satisfaction

Published by Crossway Books
a division of Good News Publishers
1300 Crescent Street
Wheaton, Illinois 60187

Cover design: Cindy Kiple

First printing 2001

Printed in the United States of America

Library of Congress Cataloging-in-Publication Data

Evans, Debra.
Soul satisfaction : for women who long for more / Debra Evans.
p. cm.
ISBN 1-58134-284-5 (pbk. : alk. paper)
1. Christian women—Religious life. I. Title.
BV4527 E893 2001
248.8'43—dc21 2001002974
CIP

15 14 13 12 11 10 09 08 07 06 05 04 03 02 01
15 1413 12 11 10 9 8 7 6 5 4 3 2 1

For my mother,

Nancy Allen Munger

joyful in worship, faithful in perseverance,
patient in prayer

CONTENTS

INTRODUCTION

My soul finds rest in God alone; my salvation comes from him. Find rest, O my soul, in God alone; my hope comes from him.

—PSALM 62:1, 5

For today's woman, the psalmist's declaration that God "satisfies the thirsty and fills the hungry with good things" (Ps. 107:9) is a revitalizing guarantee. We need to claim and cling to that promise no matter what the rugged territory around us may look like.

As you pick up *Soul Satisfaction*, I welcome you to these pages and invite you to sit down for a brief break. Perhaps you are a young woman confronting decisions concerning post-graduation plans or an older woman making the transition to retirement and beyond. Maybe you are in the midst of midlife changes as your last child leaves home or you realize the time for having children of your own is over. Possibly you are a single woman listening for God's call regarding marriage or wondering if you are becoming too isolated in your independence . . . a married woman who knows that you and your husband are not perfect and can't meet all of each other's needs and expectations . . . a mom who appreciates your need for quiet moments during the daily flow of your family's activities . . . a woman who, regardless of your current age and life stage, has found yourself recently pondering this book's topic.

Oswald Chambers once observed: "The author who benefits you most is not the one who tells you something you did not know before, but the one who gives expression to the truth that has been dumbly struggling in you for utterance."[1]

I kept these words in mind as I wrote *Soul Satisfaction* and thought about the deeply personal experiences you would bring to your reading of this book. My guess is that you are here now because you sincerely desire in some way to better articulate what you already know—not because you want me to "tell you something you did not know before." I recognize you are the real authority concerning your soul's appetites: You know better than anyone else how spiritual hunger has influenced and is affecting your life. Thus, I offer you my own thoughts and observations on this subject as a heartfelt encouragement, not as an expert, but as a companion on the journey who is wholeheartedly cheering you on.

Perhaps, like me, you recognize the tendency of your heart toward busyness, restlessness, and distraction. Maybe you, too, have discovered what it is like to long for the kind of lasting satisfaction you cannot permanently find through performing your job, furnishing a home, or fulfilling vital commitments to the people around you. In all probability you have experienced this hunger without abandoning your desire for rewarding relationships, a good marriage, meaningful work, and/or healthy children. You know firsthand what it means to be blessed by God in many varied areas in your life. Yet you still long for something more. If any of this sounds familiar to you, I urge you to keep reading.

In the pages ahead you will receive my support from the sidelines in these four ways: First, I will ask you to examine the myth that our souls can ever be completely satisfied apart from an eternal relationship with Jesus Christ. Second, I will invite you to reflect on the scope and shape of your spiritual hunger and about the ways you reach for soothing, yet ultimately unsatisfying, substitutes. Third, I will point to solid evidence showing how Christ's love can increasingly satisfy your soul's hunger by transforming your mind, changing your character, and healing your heart, if this is your desire. Finally, I will implore you to direct your soul's hunger toward Jesus—how your love for Him can be expressed moment by moment through your thoughts, deeds, and actions, enabling you to "live a life of love" (Eph. 5:2) while actively seeking to find your steady source of contentment in Christ alone.

In the following chapters you will find focus points to consider as you set aside quiet moments to examine your hunger for God. Since time is at a premium in our unquiet lives, I have tried to assist your periods of prayer, study, and reflection by drawing a variety of resources together into one lean, accessible volume. The contents of *Soul Satisfaction* are intended to act as a springboard from which you may choose to dive into a vast reservoir of Scripture and classical Christian literature, using whatever time and energy you have available.

The poems, psalms, personal stories, hymns, prayers, and book excerpts offered for your consideration lend additional support to each chapter's reading and writing activities. You may elect to do every exercise or none at all, to read the book slowly with pauses for study or straight through without stopping. Isn't it a relief to start reading *Soul Satisfaction* just because you want to? As a result, you can choose to complete or not complete any exercise or activity you find inside. I promise I will not assign you a final grade at the end of the last, or any, chapter.

It is my hope you will gain an extra measure of motivation and encouragement as you take time to think about your inner appetites, delve into the Bible, and complete these exercises. Be absolutely honest, and you may make some interesting and profitable discoveries. I suggest that you keep a personal for-your-eyes-only journal of your thoughts and reflections. There is no need to share what you learn about yourself and others unless you decide this kind of discussion will be beneficial for you. Your journal may also serve as a valuable reference point later on. (I have heard some authors, including critically acclaimed novelists, say their best-received books began in just this fashion.)

"Our Lord knows that we'll never feel fully at rest during our earthly journey. He knows that most of what we do daily to maintain our lives and much of what we do for pleasure leaves us tired," writer Sheila Cragg reminds us. "The Lord Himself is inviting us to follow Him to a place of peaceful quietness for personal restoration, to find a place of solitude for spiritual recuperation. Come, sit at the place He's set for you. He longs to serve you, so let His healing Word quench your thirst; let His tender mercy refresh your starved soul; let His gracious love awaken your spiritual passion."[2]

Jesus extends to you His clear invitation: "Here I am! I stand at the door and knock. If anyone hears my voice and opens the door, I will come in and eat with him, and he with me" (Rev. 3:20). How will you respond? Are you willing to surrender your appetites, slow down, and pay attention for a moment to your soul's keen hunger?

As you read this book and savor a portion of the Lord's divine feast, my prayer is that you will often taste the joy of Jesus' presence at His banqueting table.

He has taken me to the banquet hall,
and his banner over me is love. (Song of Songs 2:4)

Why should I call Thee LORD, Who art my God?
Why should I call Thee Friend, Who art my Love?
Or King, Who art my very Spouse above?
Or call Thy Sceptre on my heart Thy rod?
Lo now Thy banner over me is love,
All heaven flies open to me at Thy nod:
For Thou hast lit Thy flame in me a clod,
Made me a nest for dwelling of Thy Dove.
What wilt Thou call me in our home above,
Who now has called me friend? how will it be
When Thou for good wine settest forth the best?
Now Thou dost bid me come and sup with Thee,
Now Thou dost make me lean upon Thy breast:
How will it be with me in time of love?[3]

—CHRISTINA ROSSETTI (1830-1894),
"AFTER COMMUNION"

CHAPTER ONE

The Hunger We Have: *What Are We Longing For?*

You know what I long for, Lord; you hear my every sigh.

—PSALM 38:9 NLT

You have made us for yourself, and our heart is restless till it rests in you. Who will grant me to rest content in you? To whom shall I turn for the gift of your coming into my heart so that I may forget all the wrong I have done, and embrace you alone, my only good?[1]

—AUGUSTINE OF HIPPO (354-430)

Naught but God
Can satisfy the soul.[2]

—PHILIP JAMES BAILEY (1816-1902)

Every good and perfect gift is from above, coming down from the Father of the heavenly lights, who does not change like shifting shadows.

—JAMES 1:17

This is what I believe: We have been made with a persistent hunger for perfect love, the kind of love only God can give us. We were born with an intense longing for beauty, the reflection of our Creator in the breathtaking splendor of His creation. We have been designed with a deep-seated desire for using our unique talents, the ability "to do good works, which God prepared in advance for us to do" (Eph. 2:10). Whether we are single or married, rich or poor, old or young, we have been created to discover the source of our meaning, value, and identity in the character and image of Jesus Christ—in a permanent, eternal relationship with the only Man who never changes.

But here's the rub. Because God has divinely designed us to love and be loved by others, to be drawn toward breathtaking natural beauty, and to employ our unique gifts for His glory, we are prone to look for lasting satisfaction elsewhere, especially in our most important relationships with our spouses and friends, in our multiple roles as caretakers and mothers, in our varied responsibilities as coworkers and churchgoers, and in our personally focused desire to be the wise, wonderful women we were created to be.

Even though reality dictates that over time changes will occur in all of our roles and relationships and that we will encounter ongoing spiritual challenges from the moment we arrive on earth, we yearn for permanence and perfection this side of heaven. Our hearts, as Augustine observed, remain restless. We hold within our God-made design the glorious legacy of the creation, even as our souls carry the terrible imprint of the Fall.

Whether we like it or not, we are easily tempted to fasten our inner restlessness and deepest longings on things that cannot possibly satisfy our soul's hunger. We may attach our sense of self-worth to other people, a job, how we look, or what we own. We might believe that finding the right mate, stepping into a certain career, or acquiring possessions will somehow "complete" us. We sometimes think, *If only God will give me* ________ (new opportunities, a nurturing family, better health, a larger budget, less demanding kids, a higher education, greater beauty, more talent, different friends—simply fill in the blank), *then I will be* _________ (considerably happier, more content, less stressed, significantly calmer, very blessed, deeply satisfied, essentially at peace with God, myself, and the world).

But is this really true? Of course it's not. Our souls would remain hungry even if we had all of these things.

> FOCUS POINT➢ No person, no possession, no accomplishment on earth can satisfy our soul's deep hunger.

Consider for a moment what you might do if you suddenly were given twenty million dollars in cash with no strings attached and no tax due. Most of us cannot imagine having so much money we would never again have to think about paying the mortgage or the rent, saving up for college expenses or a dream vacation, or investing regularly in a retirement account. Many of us wonder what it would be like to drive a brand-new car off the lot after handing the office manager the full purchase amount in cash, or move from a rented apartment into a home of our own, or anonymously donate sizable sums to our church or favorite charity. Some of us picture finishing one year with every bill paid on time, without late penalties or overdraft fees. In summary, it is almost as challenging for most of us to think about what it would be like to have twenty thousand, two thousand, or two hundred dollars extra in our savings account as it is to imagine how our lives might change if we had twenty million dollars sitting in the bank.

I clearly remember the day three years ago when I met a man who had money to burn. I had taken an early direct flight from Austin to San Jose where my sister Kerry's husband, Dave, picked me up in his small two-seater Cessna for the brief trip

The soul on earth is an immortal guest, compelled to starve at an unreal feast; a pilgrim panting for the rest to come; an exile, anxious for his native home.

HANNAH MORE

O Lord, you have examined my heart and know everything about me.

PSALM 139:1 NLT

The one thing for which we have been created is the doing of the will of God.

JAMES S. STEWART

to a local airport near their home. For my brother-in-law flying is usually preferable to driving over the mountains along the hazardous route between the valley and the coast.

After we landed and Dave had stowed his plane, he pointed out one of his colleagues who was getting ready to take off in his new airplane, a sleek red fiberglass design built exclusively for high-performance air acrobatics. Dave then asked me if I would like to meet Kyle (a pseudonym). We walked the short distance to the spot where Dave's friend was securely strapping himself into the open cockpit of his aircraft.

The first thing to catch my attention was the elaborate safety gear required for the type of flying Kyle was about to do, including some sort of special (flame-retardant?) suit and multiple body straps with metal buckles that he tightened with a built-in ratcheting device. The second thing I noticed was Kyle's youthful appearance. I guessed he was probably thirty-two or thirty-three years of age, tops. Though Dave some months earlier had explained the situation—that Kyle and another high-tech expert had formed a small software company a few years before and had recently sold it for a net profit of forty million dollars, of which each partner received half—I was still surprised when I finally met the newly retired mogul.

Once Kyle started the plane, Dave suggested we watch him fly for several minutes. I had no idea what would happen once the plane was in the air, but I suspected something out of the ordinary was about to take place. I watched the plane taxi to the runway, make an unusually swift ascent, and head in a nearly vertical direction.

It seemed only a matter of seconds before Kyle initiated his first acrobatic maneuver, a controlled nose dive called a "death spiral" that instantly sent him plummeting earthward until he chose to reverse the situation, resume flying, and repeat the maneuver all over again.

Since I had no desire to keep watching this terrifying behavior, I have no idea how many times Kyle determinedly pointed his plane toward Watsonville's strawberry fields. As we drove away from the tiny airport and began heading north along the Pacific Coast, I took some deep breaths of the sweet-smelling ocean air and got my bearings. My recurring thought was,

So this is how someone spends his time after achieving the dream.

Here was a guy with no mortgage, college debt, or car loans left to pay—someone in his early thirties with enough wealth to indefinitely support an extremely well-cushioned existence, a man whom many people doubtless emulate and envy, and I had just seen a real-life picture of how he was investing his days by risking his life. How long would the thrill of performing death spirals last? What comes after we achieve our dreams?

The scene reminded me of these words from Ecclesiastes: "Those who love money will never have enough. How absurd to think that wealth brings true happiness! The more you have, the more people come to help you spend it. So what is the advantage of wealth—except perhaps to watch it run through your fingers! People who live only for wealth come to the end of their lives as naked and empty-handed as on the day they were born" (Eccl. 5:10-11, 15 NLT).

In reading the passage, I was also reminded of my own desires and longings regarding what money can buy. I realized how easy it is for me to miss the mark. Though I would not choose to perform daily rounds of death spirals if I suddenly came into twenty million dollars, my heart would still be at risk.

> FOCUS POINT➢ Our hunger pangs remind us of our need for God.

The myth that we can find true happiness or satisfy our deepest desires through temporary

Your hands made me and formed me; give me understanding to learn your commands.

PSALM 119:73

We are immensely significant, and our value does not depend on anything we do, think, say, feel, earn, inherit, or look like. It is because we exist as God's creation. Finis. Nothing more.

JUDITH COUCHMAN

You can't have everything. Where would you put it?

STEVEN WRIGHT

material gain, transient achievements, or time-bound relationships is at first glance a powerful idea. But if we take this attractive notion to its logical, real-life conclusion by asking ourselves, "After the dream, then what?" we soon recognize that it's not our fulfilled dreams that bring us lasting happiness and satisfaction, but the hope of *something more*.

Remember the movie *Rocky*? Though the Oscar-winning 1976 film and its overplayed theme song now seem quite outdated, who can forget its scenes of a not-yet-known actor named Sylvester Stallone sprinting up countless rows of concrete steps at the Philadelphia Art Museum, gulping down a revolting concoction of raw eggs, and pummeling his way to sudden victory in the boxing ring as his one true love, played by Talia Shire, anxiously awaited nearby? If only one version of the tale had been filmed, maybe the myth would have remained intact, but a drawn-out string of second-rate sequels revealed the steady deterioration of the main characters' lives in the first big fight's aftermath. Life for Rocky after he achieved his dream was not pretty, I assure you. Anyone remember *Rocky V*?

Personally, I prefer romantic comedies to blood-soaked slugfests any day, even though the zany situations these films portray bear practically zero resemblance to what I have experienced over thirty-one years of marriage and family life. I'm not ashamed to admit it: I enjoy watching a well-written boy-meets-girl story with plenty of preposterous humor, some unexpected plot twists, and, above all, an implausibly cheerful climax. The entertainment value of such films, at least for me, has absolutely nothing whatsoever to do with whether the characters impeccably played by Audrey, Mel, Gregory, Gwyneth, Tom, or Julia are like any of the people I know. They're not! Happy endings, I must admit, make me smile with unabashed pleasure; sad moments almost always make me cry.

Often on the way out of the theater my husband, Dave, a seasoned mental health executive, reminds me that if the fictitious situations we have just seen on the screen were to happen *in real life*, all manner of tragic consequences would eventually ensue.

"Their personal backgrounds and professional interests didn't mesh," he will say. "In real life they wouldn't stand a chance." Or, "If you take into account their conflicting social status and the time period they were living in, in real life the marriage would be doomed from the start." Or, and this is one of my favorites, "Give me a break! Once that guy showed up again at her door and the audience started clapping, why couldn't they see it would be only a matter of weeks before he would grow restless and take off down the river? In real life people don't change that easily."

Dave is right, of course. I know this. In real life people don't change that easily, and this is precisely the point. Romantic comedies and dramas showcase our collective fantasies about love, rather than the fact-based experiences we derive over whole lifetimes of loving. These stories are just barely "real" enough to make us want to believe they are true. I repeat: I know this, but I'm far from being immune to the allure of sweet dreams.

Rocky was one thing. *Emma, Pride and Prejudice*, and *Sense and Sensibility*, however, are something entirely different. (Not to mention my top twenty Most Romantic Movies of All Time, a list that includes *The Last of the Mohicans* with Daniel Day-Lewis's "I *will* find you!" declaration of devotion scene, darkly shot in golden torchlight behind a shimmering waterfall. Dave long ago abandoned trying to reason with me about this one.) I make this confession lightheartedly, of course, even as I marvel at my ongoing ability to temporarily suspend thoughtful analysis for the sake of a poignant story.

With a wide array of TV shows, ads, songs, books, magazines, and movies reinforcing the

As for God, his way is perfect; the word of the Lord is flawless.

PSALM 18:30

Lord, may no gift of Yours ever take Your place in my heart. Help me to hold them lightly in an open palm, that the supreme object of my desire may always be You and You alone.

ELISABETH ELLIOT

Inordinate love of the flesh is cruelty, because under the appearance of pleasing the body we kill the soul.

BERNARD OF CLAIRVAUX

desirability of personal success, vast wealth, and romantic love, we enjoy our dreams without believing that they will actually come true. So when we encounter appealing fictitious images and storylines, we normally know in advance we will not be buying what we see and hear hook, line, and sinker. Yet at some level, perhaps without even realizing it, we are influenced by what we see and hear if we measure our self-worth and personal satisfaction with the broken yardstick such myths provide.

> FOCUS POINT➢ Finding our identity in the character and image of Jesus Christ, through the help of His Spirit and instruction of His Word, stills our longings and satisfies our souls.

Though our self-worth is based on God's view of us, not on our own opinions or others' attitudes toward us, the culture we live in constantly bombards us with contradictory and confusing messages about our value and identity. The environment we live in is not spiritually neutral. I suspect you already have a pretty good idea of what I'm talking about and by now may be aware of the impact this culture has on your life.

Consider for a moment the dozens of monthly magazines stacked near the checkout lines at every discount store, grocery, and drugstore. What is their editors' best advice on how we can be fit, smart, elegant, sexy, and successful? A quick glance at their eye-catching covers tells us: "Nip HOLIDAY WEIGHT GAIN in the bud," "COMFORT: How to give it, feel it, wear it, feed it to your friends," "ROMANCE! LOVE! MARRIAGE!" "Why everybody's doing YOGA," "What's HOT NOW—50 must-haves for the new year," "ROSES, TRUFFLES & PASSION," "7 days to FITNESS: Our walking plan will get you there," "EMOTIONAL SPENDING: Do you need a money makeover?" "TAME THE MESS! Tricks for a Perfect Closet," "MODERN MAKEUP: It's time to play it cool," "THE RIGHT WAY TO INVEST NOW!" "GOLDEN GLOBES: Class and cleavage steal the show," and "INDULGE YOURSELF."

These sample cover blurbs are only a handful of the tamest captions. When seen in combination with countless other attention-getting headlines, plus the hundreds of pages of ads and articles inside the magazines, plus innumerable newspaper, TV, and radio advertisements, plus myriad Internet and unsolicited E-mail offerings, plus a wide assortment of book covers, posters, billboards, and bus signs . . . you get the picture.

Given our spiritual makeup and the material world we live in, it's not really surprising that women today experience varying degrees of dissatisfaction concerning their size, age, family, income, hormone levels, appearance, friends, emotional health, work load, sexuality, personal talents, menstrual patterns, history, energy level, breasts, financial status, home decor, church, daily schedules, possessions, employment expectations, physical health, living conditions, hair, time constraints, stress level, diet, retirement plans, wardrobe, social life, childbearing potential, food choices, complexion, work environment, travel opportunities, neighborhood, fitness level, wardrobe, job productivity, leisure time, spiritual health, educational experience, control level, and/or future.

It's a fact: We now have more choices, options, and opportunities than ever before. Needless to say, this is not all bad. But with the expansive array of possibilities comes the likelihood of confusion and doubt concerning who we are—our real selves—not to mention wider avenues for temptation, sin, and heartbreak. Our hearts are easily distracted. We keep searching for innovative ways to remake our imperfect selves while internally debating the benefits of new, better, improved "solutions." We are not satisfied for long.

In his excellent book, *The Divine Conspiracy*, theologian and scholar Dallas Willard poses two penetrating questions:

Remember the caution: "Beware of the barrenness of a busy life."

RUTH BELL GRAHAM

Real life is not measured by how much we own.

LUKE 12:15 NLT

Simplicity is the secret of seeing things clearly.

OSWALD CHAMBERS

The world and its desires pass away, but the man who does the will of God lives forever.

1 JOHN 2:17

> Who teaches you? Whose disciple are you? Honestly. One thing is for sure. You are somebody's disciple. You learned how to live from somebody else. There are no exceptions to this rule, for human beings are just the kind of creatures that have to learn and keep learning from others how to live. . . . It is one of the major transitions of life to recognize who has taught us, mastered us, and then to evaluate the results in us of their teaching. This is a harrowing task, and sometimes we just can't face it. But it can also open the door to other masters, possibly better masters, and one Master above all.[3]

Making Christ our Master means letting go of our fears and anxieties related to what others have taught us about who we are; it requires recognizing, recalling, and reminding ourselves of what will satisfy us, where we will find sustenance, and whom we will "seek first." "Your heavenly Father already knows all your needs," Jesus proclaimed, "and he will give you all you need from day to day if you live for him and make the Kingdom of God your primary concern" (Matt. 6:32-33 NLT).

Commitment to Christ requires single-mindedness—the kind of devotion and obedience that can only be produced by the Holy Spirit working in our lives. As the Spirit increases our hunger for the Bread of Life and leads us into a deeper awareness of Christ's lordship, our thoughts, feelings, and desires come more completely under His divine authority. Then the Spirit's fruit—love, joy, peace, patience, kindness, goodness, faithfulness, gentleness, and self-control—can be produced within us and experienced in greater abundance. Thus our single-mindedness becomes a hidden source of soul-preserving protection.

As our hearts are focused on God's kingdom and our minds are set on Christ, our hungry souls are strengthened, sustained, and shielded from harm. Day by day we can lift our souls to the Lord of life, asking Him to lead us, feed us, fortify us, and make us more fruitful: "Fill my cup, Lord—I lift it up, Lord! Come and quench the thirsting of my soul; Bread of Heaven, feed me till I want no more—Fill my cup, fill it up and make me whole!"[4]

How much we need to hear and heed Jesus' promise that He will strengthen us for the journey ahead and light our way with His unfailing love, grace, and protection. By feeding on God's Word, we gain much-needed strength and the ability to conform to His will. As we feast on His daily provision, our hope and faith increase.

"You have made known to me the path of life; you will fill me with joy in your presence, with eternal pleasures at your right hand," declared David (Ps. 16:11). But we must take time to pray, to wait, to listen. Nothing is more important than this. Nothing will fill and satisfy our souls until they find their rest in the joy of Jesus' unfailing love.

Reality, reality,
Lord Jesus Christ, Thou art to me!
From the spectral mist and the driving clouds,
From the shifting shadows and phantom crowds,
From unreal words and unreal lives,
Where truth with falsehood feebly strives;
From the passings away, the chance and change,
Flickerings, vanishings, swift and strange,
I turn to my glorious rest in Thee,
Who art the grand Reality!

Reality, reality,
In the brightest days Thou art to me!
Thou art the sunshine of my mirth;
Thou art the heaven above my earth,
The spring of love of all my heart,
And the fountain of my song Thou art;
For dearer than the dearest now,
And better than the best art Thou,
Beloved Lord, in whom I see
Joy-giving, glad Reality.

Reality, reality,
Lord Jesus Christ, is crowned in Thee;
In Thee is every type fulfilled;

Money never made a man happy yet, nor will it. There is nothing in its nature to produce happiness. The more a man has, the more he wants. Instead of its filling a vacuum, it makes one. If it satisfies one want, it doubles and trebles that want another way. That was a true proverb of the wise man, rely upon it: "Better is little with the fear of the Lord than great treasure, and trouble therewith."

BENJAMIN FRANKLIN

In Thee is every yearning stilled
For perfect beauty, truth and love;
For Thou art always far above
The grandest glimpse of our Ideal;
Yet more and more we know Thee real,
And marvel more and more to see
Thine infinite Reality.[5]

—FRANCES RIDLEY HAVERGAL (1836-1879),
FROM "REALITY"

Focus Points

➢ No person, no possession, no accomplishment on earth can satisfy our soul's deep hunger.

➢ Our hunger pangs remind us of our need for God.

➢ Finding our identity in the character and image of Jesus Christ, through the help of His Spirit and instruction of His Word, stills our longings and satisfies our souls.

Nourishment from God's Word

Come, all you who are thirsty,
come to the waters;
and you who have no money,
come, buy and eat!
Come, buy wine and milk
without money and without cost.
Why spend money on what is not bread,
and your labor on what does not satisfy?
Listen, listen to me, and eat what is good,
and your soul will delight in the richest of fare.
Give ear and come to me;
hear me, that your soul may live.

—ISAIAH 55:1-4

Do not store up for yourselves treasures on earth, where moth and rust destroy, and where thieves break in and steal. But store up for yourselves treasures in heaven, where moth and rust do not destroy, and where thieves do not break in and steal. For where your treasure is, there your heart will be also.

The eye is the lamp of the body. If your eyes are good, your whole body will be full of light. But if your eyes are bad, your whole body will be full of darkness. If then light within you is darkness, how great is that darkness!

No one can serve two masters. Either he will hate the one and love the other, or he will be devoted to the one and despise the other. You cannot serve both God and Money.

Therefore I tell you, do not worry about your life, what you will eat or drink; or about your body, what you will wear. Is not life more important than food, and the body more important than clothes? Look at the birds of the air; they do not sow or reap or store away in barns, and yet your heavenly Father feeds them. Are you not more valuable than they? Who of you by worrying can add a single hour to his life?

—MATTHEW 6:19-27

How lovely is your dwelling place, O Lord Almighty!
My soul yearns, even faints, for the courts of the Lord;
my heart and my flesh cry out for the living God.
Even the sparrow has found a home, and the swallow a nest for herself,
where she may have her young—a place near your altar,
O Lord Almighty, my King and my God.
Blessed are those who dwell in your house; they are ever praising you.
Blessed are those whose strength is in you,
who have set their hearts on pilgrimage.
As they pass through the Valley of Baca, they make it a place of springs;
the autumn rains also cover it with pools.
They go from strength to strength, till each appears before God in Zion.
Hear my prayer, O Lord God Almighty; listen to me, O God of Jacob.
Look upon our shield, O God; look with favor on your anointed one.
Better is one day in your courts than a thousand elsewhere;
I would rather be a doorkeeper in the house of my God
than dwell in the tents of the wicked.
For the Lord God is a sun and shield; the Lord bestows favor and honor;

no good thing does he withhold from those whose walk is blameless.
O Lord Almighty, blessed is the man who trusts in you.

—PSALM 84

REFLECTION POINTS

1. My innermost hunger can best be described as . . .
2. For me the greatest challenge to paying attention to my soul's deepest longings lies in . . .
3. Identity can best be described as . . .
4. My sense of self-worth is most affected by . . .
5. When I don't get good spiritual nourishment, I feel . . .
6. I am most aware of my desire for "something more" when . . .
7. My own attempts at satisfying my soul's hunger often end up . . .

ADDITIONAL STUDY

—*MEDITATE ON* Psalms 63; 84; 139; Isaiah 55; John 6:25-40.

—*READ ABOUT* the desires expressed by these biblical women:

Sarah, Abraham's gorgeous wife and Isaac's surprised mother, in Genesis 16:1-6 and 21:1-13 and Hebrews 11:11-12

The *woman at the well,* a curious Samaritan with five ex-husbands, John 4:7-42

Martha, Mary's and Lazarus's too-stressed-to-be-blessed sister, in Luke 10:38-42

—*STUDY* Psalm 104:14-35; Proverbs 4:20-27; Ecclesiastes 5:10-20; Matthew 6:19-34; Luke 14:15-23; Philippians 4:14-19; 1 Peter 1:2-10.

—*MEMORIZE* Psalm 61:1; Psalm 145:15-19; Song of Songs 2:4; Matthew 5:3; James 1:17; Revelation 3:20.

SUGGESTED EXERCISES

- Make a personalized recording of the music that encourages you to draw closer to God. Take time to sit down and listen to your favorite songs, hymns, soundtracks, and/or classical compositions as you go. Play this tape or CD often in the coming weeks.

- Write a spiritual autobiography. Start with your earliest memories—your first prayers, thoughts about God, family experiences, religious books and TV shows, holiday highlights, Bible teaching, and church influences, for example. Continue your detailed narrative to the present, considering questions such as: How have the people around you at various points in your life encouraged or discouraged your interest in God? Was there a particular turning point in your life when you became more interested in knowing and following Christ? Has the Bible played an important role in your spiritual development? At what times have you been most aware of your soul's yearnings? How have you expressed these desires? From whom have you received the most valuable Christian instruction, prayer support, and guidance? What have you learned about your soul's hunger and how it may be satisfied or stifled? Conclude your autobiography with a description of your desires concerning your future spiritual growth.
- Reflect on the ways money, romance, and vocational achievement have influenced your life and the priority you have attached to each—measured by the amount of time, thought, energy, and other personal resources you have invested in these areas. Express your thoughts on this topic in your journal.
- Think about a dream you have achieved. What happened in your life as a result? Do you have a different dream now? How might your life be different if you achieve this dream? How is your life influenced today by the hopes and plans you have in relation to your dream?

Closing Prayer

Almighty God, we give Thee thanks for the mighty yearning of the human heart, for the coming of a Savior, and the constant promise of Thy Word that He was to come. In our own souls we repeat the humble sighs and panting aspirations of ancient men and ages, and own that our souls are in darkness and infirmity without faith in Him who comes to bring God to man and man to God. We bless Thee for the tribute we can pay to Him from our very sense of need and dependence, and that our own hearts can so answer, from their wilderness, the cry, "Prepare ye the way of the Lord." In us the rough places are to be made smooth, the crooked straight, the mountains of pride brought low, and the valleys of despondency lifted up. O God, prepare Thou the way in us now, and may we welcome anew Thy Holy Child. Hosanna! blessed be He who cometh in the name of the Lord — Amen.[6]

—SAMUEL OSGOOD (1812-1880)

> *I say to myself, "The LORD is my portion; therefore I will wait for him. The LORD is good to those whose hope is in him, to the one who seeks him; it is good to wait quietly for the salvation of the LORD. (Lamentations 3:24-26)*

FOOD FOR THOUGHT

He wandered along the bank of the river till he came to the foot of the hill on which stood the old castle. Seeing a gate a little further off, he went to it, and finding it open and unattended, went in. A slow-ascending drive went through the trees and round and round the hill, along which he took his way through the aromatic air that now blew and now paused as he went. Between the boles of the trees which seemed to be climbing up to attack the fortress above, he could see some of its lower windows, looking like those of cellars. When he had gone a little way out of sight of the gate, he threw himself down among the trees, and fell into a deep reverie.

The ancient time arose before him, when, without a tree to cover the approach of an enemy, the fortress rose defiant and bare in its strength, like an athlete stripped for the fight, and the little town clustered close under its protection. What wars had there blustered, what rumors blown, what fears whispered, what sorrows moaned! But were there not as many things loud and boisterous and hard to bear now as then? Did not many an evil seem now as insurmountable as then? The world will change only as the heart of man changes. Growing intellect, growing civilization will heal man's wounds only to cause the deeper ill to break out afresh in new forms, nor can they satisfy one longing of the human soul. Its desires are deeper than the soul itself, whence it groans with the groanings that cannot be uttered.

As much in the times of civilization as in those of barbarity the soul needs an external presence to make its life a good to it. In the rougher times of violence men were less conscious of the need than in our own. Time itself—starving, vacant, unlovely time—is to many the one dread foe they have to encounter. Others have the awful consciousness of a house empty and garnished in which neither Love nor Hope dwell, but doors and windows lie open to what evil things may enter. To others the very knowledge of self, with no God to protect from it, a self unrulable, insatiable, makes existence a hell. For Godless man is a horror of the unfinished, a hopeless necessity for the unattainable, in which arise and revel monstrous dreams of truest woe. Money, ease, honor, can help nothing: the most discontented are of those who have all that the truthless heart desires.[7]

—GEORGE MACDONALD (1824-1905),
FROM *DONAL GRANT*

CHAPTER TWO

THE JUNK FOOD WE EAT:
Why Aren't We Satisfied?

O God, you are my God, earnestly I seek you; my soul thirsts for you, my body longs for you, in a dry and weary land where there is no water.

—PSALM 63:1

The great danger facing all of us is not that we shall make an absolute failure of life, nor that we shall fall into outright viciousness, nor that we shall be terribly unhappy, nor that we shall feel that life has no meaning at all—not these things. The danger is that we may fail to perceive life's greatest meaning, fall short of its highest good, miss its deepest and most abiding happiness, be unable to render the most needed service, be unconscious of life ablaze with the light of the Presence of God—and be content to have it so—that is the danger. That some day we may wake up and find that always we have been busy with the husks and trappings of life—and have really missed life itself.[1]

—PHILLIPS BROOKS (1835-1893)

Unhappiness on earth cultivates a hunger for heaven. By gracing us with a deep dissatisfaction, God holds our attention.[2]

—MAX LUCADO

Have you ever experienced a feeling of fatigued emptiness as you hurried to meet another deadline, rushed to your fourth appointment of the day, answered another necessary phone call, or woke up on Monday morning after an over-packed weekend? Do you know what it is like to feel so "dry" you find yourself suddenly short-tempered and irritable in spite of your best intentions?

"Eternally, woman spills herself away in driblets to the thirsty, seldom being allowed the time, the quiet, the peace, to let the pitcher fill up to the brim," wrote Anne Morrow Lindbergh, wife of Charles Lindbergh, mother of six, and daughter of a diplomat, in *Gift from the Sea*. "We are aware of our hunger and our needs, but still ignorant of what will satisfy them. With our garnered free time, we are more apt to drain our creative springs rather than refill them. With our pitchers, we attempt sometimes to water a field, not a garden. We throw ourselves indiscriminately into committees and causes. Not knowing how to feed the spirit, we try to muffle its demands and distractions."[3]

The hectic pace we so easily fall into calls for persistent reevaluation. Meeting our basic requirements, such as activity and rest, talking and listening, serving others and spending time alone with God, is dependent on our willingness to sensibly weigh our wants and needs. Finding a healthy balance, and maintaining it, is an ongoing challenge; neglecting or denying our ongoing need for this balance can turn productive lives into parched wastelands.

Even as I write these words, I realize: Real life does not arrive in neatly wrapped packages marked "Things I Will Do Today." In any given twenty-four-hour period we may find ourselves facing more than a few minor interruptions, not to mention having loads of tasks turn out to be considerably more time-consuming and complex than we anticipated. Traffic delays, a thunderstorm, or an infected tooth can divert the day's smooth-flowing course of events into a clogged channel of hassle, full of unwelcome twists and turns—to say nothing of the truly big obstacles that occasionally come barreling our way.

Some days, some months, some years are considerably less difficult to navigate than others. For example, during the past month my schedule has been briefly rerouted along several scenic detours by a long list of unanticipated delays and last-minute decisions including, but not limited to, a rear-end collision (not my fault), Valentine's Day celebrations (fun), and recurring hormonal irregularities (not fun); numerous doctors' appointments (annoying), media interviews (invigorating), family members' birthdays (expected), and invitation-only formal dinners (unexpected); out-of-town-guests (enjoyable), seasonal allergies (unavoidable), and the President's Day Sidewalk Sale (completely avoidable).

This morning, on the last day of February, I had to phone the plumber. After diagnosing the source of our kitchen sink leak, he said that because the leak is located under a concrete slab, the job will cost four times more than previously predicted and will take considerably longer to do. As the clock ticks toward midnight, I am wondering if the month of March will bring clear skies and calm weather.

Though I am genuinely thankful nothing happened this month that would come close to qualifying as a full-blown crisis, planned and unplanned surprises like these all too often direct my time, energy, and attention away from my charted schedule. Is it only I, or do you also find yourself growing inwardly emptier while steering through rapidly changing waters?

"To learn sense is true self-love," noted Solomon (Prov. 19:8 NEB). Yet we too often get caught up in consuming *non*sense—in the spiritual

We can make our plans, but the Lord determines our steps.

PROVERBS 16:9 NLT

Growth begins when we start to accept our own weakness.

JEAN VANIER

The hope of Jesus Christ is never a dash of pepper or a spoonful of mustard. It is bread and wine, without which there is only the delirium of knowledge and an illusion of action.

JACQUES ELLUL

equivalent of junk food—because of our tendency to choose ultimately unsatisfying substitutes for God's good nourishment.

Why do we think we can keep going without harming ourselves as we rush from one person, place, project, or purchase to another—from one hour, day, week, month, or year to the next—without paying closer attention to what our hunger pangs are telling us? Again, am I the only one facing these challenges and dangers regarding my soul's health—or am I correct in assuming you too know what I'm talking about?

It's not surprising that our multifaceted roles and responsibilities demand concentrated effort, patient endurance, and more than a few calories. What is surprising, however, is how often we continue surging forward, full speed ahead, when we sincerely need to stop long enough to receive life-giving nourishment and rest, or when we try running on empty even though our souls start experiencing unhealthy cravings. Our innermost hunger can help us if we heed it.

In the seventeenth century Francis Quarles wrote, "In having all things but Thee, what have I? Not having Thee, what have my labors got? Let me enjoy but Thee, what further crave I? And having Thee alone, what have I not?"[4]

Indeed, if we belong to Jesus and His Spirit has found a home in our hearts, what do we lack? As we take time out to taste Christ's eternal bounty, what further do we crave except more of *Him*? Still, it's amazingly easy to dismiss this vital truth if our schedules begin to overflow with stressful activity, drain our inner reserves, and cause us to grow weary with life's complex demands.

> FOCUS POINT➢ Given the reality of our spiritual makeup and the amount of stress, strain, and soul-deadening diversions daily confronting us, we need ample amounts of spiritual food.

I can't help but wonder: Is the hunger we continually feel for *something more* in so many areas of our lives in truth God's gift to us, a potent earthly reminder of the spiritual nature of our soul's hunger?

Soul satisfaction begins at the place where we risk surrendering our lives to Someone we know by heart but can't touch, feel, or see with our eyes on this side of heaven. Slowing down long enough to savor our Shepherd's loving provision requires our receptive awareness to His leading. For it's only when we slow down, stop, and allow ourselves to feel the silent ache of our souls' appetite, when we choose not to dull our senses or deaden the impact of this nagging inner hunger, when we refuse to turn away from God and instead offer ourselves to His Son for help and healing and wholeness, that our deepest longings for *something more* become transformed.

Why is it sometimes so difficult for us to do this? Developing a healthy respect for the various kinds of cravings we experience, identifying the types of spiritual junk food we eat, and making comparisons between soul and body hunger can help us recognize the importance of obtaining the spiritual food with which He feeds and fuels our whole being. Consider, for example, the numerous ways our spiritual "eating" might be compared to the physical act of eating described here by the renowned food writer M. F. K. Fisher:

> Any normal man must nourish his body by means of food put into it through his mouth. This process takes time, quite apart from the lengthy preparations and digestions that accompany it.
>
> Between the ages of twenty and fifty, John Doe spends some twenty thousand hours chewing and swallowing food, more than eight hundred days and nights of steady eating. The mere contemplation of this fact is upsetting enough!

To escape the distress caused by regret for the past or fear about the future, this is the rule to follow: leave the past to the infinite mercy of God, the future to His good providence; give the present wholly to His love by being faithful to His grace.

JEAN-PIERRE DE CAUSSADE

I am the bread that came down from heaven.

JOHN 6:41

My cup overflows with blessings.

PSALM 23:5 NLT

> To some men it is actively revolting. They devise means of accomplishing the required nourishments of their bodies by pills of condensed victuals and easily swallowed draughts which equal, they are told, the food value of a beefsteak or a vegetable stew.
>
> To others, the stunning realization of how much time is needed to feed themselves is accepted more philosophically. They agree with La Rochefoucauld's aphorism: "To eat is a necessity, but to eat intelligently is an art . . . ."
>
> Whichever school a man may adhere to, the protestant or the philosophical, he continues to eat through the middle years of life with increasing interest. He grows more conscious of his body as it grows less tolerant.
>
> No longer can he dine heavily at untoward hours, filling his stomach with the adolescent excitations of hot sauces and stodgy pastries—no longer, that is, with impunity. No more can he say with any truth: "Oh, I can eat anything. I can drink without showing it. I am made of iron . . . ."
>
> But we must grow old, and we must eat. It seems far from unreasonable, once these facts are accepted, for a man to set himself the pleasant task of educating his palate so that he can do the former not grudgingly and in spite of the latter, but easily and agreeably because of it.[5]

M. F. K. Fisher's observations, first published in 1937, seem practically prophetic. She appears to have had some inkling as to what the twenty-first century would bring regarding "the art of eating"—the widespread acceptance of diet products, record sales of prepackaged food supplements, mushrooming restaurant growth, fast food burgers by the billions, and nutrition on the run.

Today bigger-sized combos, drive-through taco plates, and happy hamburger meals regularly give us a break from cooking at home—and also from sitting down together around our dining table or thoughtfully savoring our food. Thin-fast soy shakes, mega-vitamin supplements, fruit-based smoothies, and high-fiber energy bars (with fifteen grams of protein, no less) offer us the pleasure of knowing we have saved time while swallowing something healthy—and also convince us we have sacrificed nothing very important by adopting a grab-and-go lifestyle.

Has our increasing abandonment of "eating intelligently" for the sake of saving time influenced our daily spiritual intake patterns as well? I ask you, how could it not? There is no doubt in my mind that our current cultural bent toward fast and easy eating solutions often causes us to approach God, our loved ones, and ourselves with one eye always on the clock, not to mention the myriad fast, easy, and convenient ways we approach partaking of God's good food. And still we expect to experience real spiritual satisfaction—without first educating our spiritual palates as to what it means to truly taste, savor, chew, swallow, and digest God's bounty.

No matter if all the world rejects you, His word of affirmation is enough. We must learn to live our lives looking for that word.

JILL BRISCOE

To paraphrase M. F. K. Fisher, as Christ's followers today, we too have "devised means of accomplishing the required spiritual nourishment of our bodies by pills of condensed victuals and easily swallowed draughts which equal, we are told, the food value of a beefsteak or a vegetable stew." We enjoy the time-saving, regularly scheduled convenience of choosing how, when, and in what form we will receive spiritual food. Many of us expect to be adequately nourished by once-a-week doses of God's Word via a twenty-minute sermon on Sunday mornings; listening to a Christian radio talk show discussion of salvation; or reading a best-selling book focused on a single Bible verse. Like an easily swallowed liquid food supplement or a fully loaded vitamin capsule, these things can provide us with essential spiritual nutrients. But when it comes to being fed the Bread of Life, there is a big difference between our supplementary eating prac-

Why spend money on what is not bread, and your labor on what does not satisfy? Listen, listen to me, and eat what is good, and your soul will delight in the richest of fare.

ISAIAH 55:2

tices and the delightful dining experiences we are invited to privately share with our Lord. How can we expect to reach a deeper, wider, richer, more fulfilling level of soul satisfaction without first educating our spiritual palates and developing our desire to truly taste, savor, chew, swallow, and digest our spiritual food?

Eating, whether it takes place on the spiritual or the physical level, takes time. Tasting and savoring takes time. Chewing and swallowing takes time. Digesting takes time. But time is at a premium in our busy lives. So to save time we have learned many different ways to eat, both physically and spiritually, that do not require that we quietly sit down and *taste* our food as we eat, chew, swallow, and digest it.

We eat while we drive to work, school, or an appointment. We eat while we read a book, magazine, or newspaper. We eat while we watch TV, browse the Internet, or go out to a movie. We eat while we hold a business, board, or church meeting. We eat while we cheer our favorite football, baseball, basketball, or hockey team to victory. We eat while we converse near a buffet table or hear a featured banquet speaker. Rarely do we take the time to prepare a complete, nutritious meal and then sit down, knife and fork in hand, taking time to fully taste what we eat, savoring each bite to the fullest, chewing slowly, swallowing consciously, feeling the pleasure of satisfying our hunger, and then resting as digestion gradually takes place.

Junk food, both natural and supernatural, is an appealing, even addictive, substitute for real food. We do not eat high-calorie, low-nutrient food because it is actually *good* for us, right? We eat our favorite junk food because our previously conditioned appetites produce an almost irresistible craving for a quick snack. We choose junk food because we like the way it momentarily makes us feel on the inside, in spite of how it may eventually make us look on the outside. Sometimes we choose it even when we are not really hungry, or when we know better, or when we already know that junk food does not ultimately satisfy us.

Perhaps it would help if we considered "junk food" to be something more than merely "high-calorie food with few recommended daily nutrients." Maybe physical/spiritual junk food is actually *any* food we do not value enough to eat mindfully, consciously, or thankfully—food eaten simply because we know we have to eat, food consumed during the course of the day with little to no thought for God's amazing provision. Most importantly, doesn't the term "junk food," regardless of the way we define it, imply that our bodies are similar to garbage cans?

Comparisons between the ways we try to satisfy our physical hunger and our spiritual hunger reveal additional striking similarities. For example, if we eat a huge meal, we shouldn't expect to feel full two days later. If we consistently eat too much, our hunger is masked and medicated—we miss feeling hunger as a healthy signal, gain weight or purge ourselves, no longer receive needed nutrients, and rely on our own judgment instead of our bodies' natural rhythms. If we eat and drink the wrong things, we get sick. If we don't eat or drink anything at all, we begin to starve. Without enough vitamins, minerals, protein, carbohydrates, water, and calories our bodies begin to wither, become diseased, and waste away.

Likewise, if we attend church on Sunday and neglect our spiritual needs on Monday and Tuesday, we shouldn't expect to function well spiritually two days later. If we overwork ourselves, our faith is no longer fresh and vibrant—we miss seeing the obvious, grow in pride or become self-critical, push ourselves to keep going, and rely on our own strength instead of the Holy Spirit. If we break God's commandments and ignore His Word, our souls get sick. If we deny our need of God and don't actively seek Him, our souls begin

Do not despair of yourselves. You are men, made in the image of God, and He who made you was Himself made man; the blood of the only begotten Son was shed for you. If, thinking of your frailty, you hold yourselves cheap, value yourselves by the price that was paid for you.

St. Augustine

When you get to your wit's end, you'll find God lives there.

Elizabeth Yates

to starve. Without enough prayer, reflection on God's Word, obedience to Christ's commands, receptivity and responsiveness to the Holy Spirit's inner working, fellowship with other believers, and quiet rest in the Lord's strengthening presence, our souls begin to wither, become diseased, and waste away.

On a physical level, our aversion to sitting down quietly at the table and eating with focused awareness doesn't seem so much a rejection of the pleasure of eating as a desire for ease and efficiency. We pack so many things into each day we often are too tired to create a satisfying meal or too rushed to reflect upon what we taste. We hurriedly devour a candy or granola bar for instant energy, gulp down a quick cup of coffee or a Coke to stay awake, chomp on a carrot or foil-wrapped Cajun chicken sandwich with our free hand gripping the steering wheel. And so it is with God's good nourishment for our souls: We may think we can squeeze in our daily quiet time with Jesus while rushing en route to the next appointment or finishing up in the bathroom—while sitting on the toilet, no less—and still be well-nourished by the Bread of Life.

Contrast this kind of careless eating with a different kind of dining experience. Picture yourself arriving at a close friend's dinner party. Upon walking in the front door, you are immediately surrounded by a concentrated blend of favorite aromas—freshly baked bread; pumpkin pie; roast turkey stuffed with sage dressing; steaming cider mulled with cinnamon, orange peel, and cloves; homemade applesauce, and sweet potato casserole just out of the oven.

Your hostess has put out her best dishes on an antique lace tablecloth. Each place has been set with hand-embroidered napkins, gleaming flatware, and tall, iced goblets filled with lemon slices and water. In the center of the table a shallow cut-glass bowl holds a welcoming arrangement of autumn-colored flowers. Flickering candles make everything appear softer.

When it is time to eat, the guests gather around the table, talking and laughing, and sit down. A quiet hush falls over the group as heads are bowed, and each person takes the hands of neighbors. No one is in a hurry to eat, except for the toddler down at the end squirming momentarily in his highchair. With praise and thanksgiving, after a few heartfelt prayers have been said, all join in singing the family's traditional song with enthusiastic delight.

The meal is served. You take just enough to enjoy your selected portions. Every bite you chew brings a bright burst of flavor, filling your nose and mouth with each food's remarkable characteristics. You never realized you could actually enjoy eating fresh Brussels sprouts. Yet this dish (what did she put in it?) has convinced you to forget your longstanding prejudice against this particular vegetable.

After dabbing some real butter on a still-warm yeast roll, you take a taste, chewing the bread slowly. You think about the bread. . . .

> FOCUS POINT➢ Our spiritual health is promoted when we choose to live wisely by paying attention to the way God has designed us.

As you may have already discovered, spiritual junk food comes in all shapes, textures, colors, and sizes. It can be spicy or mild, smooth or crunchy, sweet or sour, bland or salty. We're ultimately our own producers of the spiritual junk food we eat because it is *the fruit of our own thoughts, attitudes, beliefs, and behaviors*. (You may want to take a moment later and make a list of behaviors that produce your spiritual junk food. I'm guessing that if you are already familiar with the Bible, many of the things on your list will either match or resemble many of the items on mine. After completing

He who comes to me will never go hungry, and he who believes in me will never be thirsty.

JOHN 6:35

He does not force our wills but only takes what we give Him, but He does not give Himself entirely until He sees that we yield ourselves entirely to Him.

TERESA OF AVILA

I run in the path of your commands, for you have set my heart free.

PSALM 119:32

your list, I invite you to turn to the last page of this chapter and determine if my hunch is correct. No cheating, of course.)

In increasingly surrendering our lives to Christ and desiring His sweet companionship above everything and everyone else, our souls are nourished and revived. What a far cry this is from the wow-this-sure-tastes-good-now-but-just-wait-until-later kind of nourishment we feed our souls when we try to meet our innermost cravings with spiritual junk food!

Fortunately, we aren't satisfied by spiritual substitutes for long. Our God-given nature creates a persistent hunger inside our souls for the Bread of Life—for the delightful sustenance we receive when we "sit down at the table" with Christ and take time to enjoy, savor, and feast upon His presence. Over the course of our lives, *God helps us to keep turning toward Him alone for satisfaction*, teaching us why, how, and where to look for the one kind of food that really matters.

But to become aware of our inner need for this good food and to live with the anticipation of receiving *something more* as God's gift, we must, by God's mercy, offer our very selves to him: "a living sacrifice, dedicated and fit for his acceptance, the worship offered by mind and heart" (Rom. 12:1 NEB).

"Jesus promised to fill those who hunger and thirst after righteousness," contemporary theologian Dr. R. C. Sproul points out. "He made no promise to fill those who are not hungry."[6] Is this why our soul's hunger cannot be filled? Why our repeated attempts to relieve our inner discontent through self-help cures never really work? Clearly, our soul's ongoing hunger is one of the ways God providentially points us in His direction, and we find in the Bible no shortage of references to physical hunger and satisfaction as a means of teaching us about the vital spiritual sustenance we can receive only from the Lord.

"What we find in the lives and writings of the great saints is the elusive 'something more' often promised by lesser preachers, but rarely found by casual observers," says Dr. Sproul. "Is there really something more?" he asks. "Is there a level of Christian faith and devotion higher than the commonplace? Is there a state of the soul that involves more rest than restlessness? The answer to all these questions is an emphatic *yes*!"[7]

FOCUS POINT➢ Desiring Christ above everything and everyone else is neither effortless nor automatic.

Bernard of Clairvaux was one of those astonishing saints whose writing reveals his tender yearning for the elusive *something more*, a faith and devotion higher than the commonplace, the state of a soul that involved more rest than restlessness. In his classic treatise titled *The Love of God*, Bernard poignantly pronounces:

> Every rational person naturally desires to be always satisfied with what it esteems preferable. It is never satisfied with something that lacks the qualities it desires to have. So if a man has chosen a wife because of her beauty, then he will look out with a roving eye for more beautiful women. Or if he is desirous of being well dressed, he will look out for even more expensive clothes. No matter how rich he is, if wealth is his desire, he will envy those who are richer than he is. . . . men in high places are drawn on by insatiable ambitions to climb higher and higher still. Indeed, there is no end to all this, because unsatisfied desires have no final satisfaction if they cannot be defined as absolutely the best or the highest.
>
> Need we wonder then that a man cannot find contentment with what is less or worse since he seeks peace and satisfaction in what is highest and best? So how stupid and mad it is to seek to find peace or satisfaction in that which cannot fulfill these needs. So no mat-

You must remember that our God has all knowledge and all wisdom, and that therefore it is very possible He may guide you into paths wherein He knows great blessings are awaiting you, but which, to the shortsighted human eyes around you, seem sure to result in confusion and loss.

HANNAH WHITALL SMITH

Unless we identify the true source of human desire, our desires will remain unfulfilled.

JAMES HOUSTON

> ter how many things one may possess, he will always be lusting for what is perceived to be still missing. Discontented, he will spend himself in restlessness and futility. Thus the restless heart runs to and fro looking for the pleasures of this life in weariness of the evanescent and the unreal. He is like a starving man who thinks anything he can stuff down his throat is not enough, for his eyes are still looking at what he has not eaten. Thus man craves continually for what is still lacking, with more anxiety in his preoccupation with what he lacks rather than having any joy or contentment in what he has already got. . . .
>
> Rest in God alone. Man experiences no real peace in this world, but he has no restlessness to disturb him in the eternal state with God. Thus the soul can say with confidence, "It is good for me to draw near to God. . . . Whom have I in heaven but Thee; and there is none upon earth that I desire beside Thee. . . . God is the strength of my heart and my portion forever (Psalm 73:28, 25, 26). Therefore, as I have said, even coming by this way of trying out all lesser goods one after the other, this may eventually drive us to realize that it is God alone who can truly satisfy.[8]

Will we "learn sense" as Solomon advised and thereby resist consuming the abundant empty calories daily offered us? Taking enough time to satisfy our hunger for Living Bread—whether this means going alone to our preferred quiet place, or praying in bed when we lie awake in the middle of the night, or sitting in solitude at the kitchen table when the room is no longer noisy—supplies us with hidden sustenance for the hours ahead.

"Taste and see that the LORD is good," David's psalm invites us. "Oh, the joys of those who trust in him!" (Ps. 34:8 NLT). We don't have to wait until tomorrow to seek and find the source of our soul's satisfaction. When we want to learn how to taste the Lord's goodness, we don't need to develop a special diet plan, enroll in a complicated nutritional program, read dozens of cookbooks, or pay a hefty fee. We can begin right here, with what we have on hand, as we sit quietly before the Lord with open hearts, waiting to receive His perfect provision. We can start educating our soul's palate today, one meal at a time, as we dine at our Savior's table, desiring to fully taste and see that the Lord indeed is *good*.

Jesus, Thou Joy of loving hearts,
Thou Fount of life, Thou Light of men,
From the best bliss that earth imparts,
We turn unfilled to Thee again.

Thy truth unchanged has ever stood,
Thou savest those that on Thee call;
To them that seek Thee, Thou are good,
To them that find Thee, all in all.

We taste Thee, O Thou Living Bread,
And long to feast upon Thee still;
We drink of Thee, the Fountainhead,
And thirst our souls from Thee to fill.

Our restless spirits long for Thee,
Where'er our changeful lot is cast;
Glad when Thy gracious smile we see,
Blest when our faith can hold Thee fast.

O Jesus, ever with us stay,
Make all our moments calm and bright;
Chase the dark night of sin away,
Shed o'er the world Thy holy light.

—BERNARD OF CLAIRVAUX
(1091-1153)

Focus Points

➢ Given the reality of our spiritual makeup and the amount of stress, strain, and soul-deadening diversions daily confronting us, we need ample amounts of spiritual food.

➢ Our spiritual health is promoted when we choose to live wisely, by paying attention to the way God has designed us.

➢ Desiring Christ above everything and everyone else is neither effortless nor automatic.

Nourishment from God's Word

Yes, he humbled you by letting you go hungry and then feeding you with manna, a food previously unknown to you and your ancestors. He did it to teach you that people need more than bread for their life; real life comes by feeding on every word of the LORD.

—DEUTERONOMY 8:3 NLT

Then they asked him, "What must we do to do the works God requires?"

Jesus answered, "The work of God is this: to believe in the one he has sent."

So they asked him, "What miraculous sign then will you give that we may see it and believe you? What will you do? Our forefathers ate the manna in the desert; as it is written: 'He gave them bread from heaven to eat.'"

Jesus said to them, "I tell you the truth, it is not Moses who has given you the bread from heaven, but it is my Father who gives you the true bread from heaven. For the bread of God is he who comes down from heaven and gives life to the world."

"Sir," they said, "from now on give us this bread."

Then Jesus declared, "I am the bread of life. He who comes to me will never go hungry, and he who believes in me will never be thirsty . . . . Your forefathers ate the manna in the desert, yet they died. But here is the bread that comes down from heaven, which a man may eat and not die. I am the living bread that came down from heaven. If anyone eats of this bread, he will live forever. This bread is my flesh, which I will give for the life of the world."

—JOHN 6:28-35, 49-51

The LORD is gracious and compassionate,
forbearing, and constant in his love.
The LORD is good to all men,
and his tender care rests upon all his creatures.
All thy creatures praise thee, LORD, and thy servants bless thee.
They talk of the glory of thy kingdom and tell of thy might,
they proclaim to their fellows how mighty are thy deeds,
how glorious the majesty of thy kingdom.
Thy kingdom is an everlasting kingdom,
and thy dominion stands for all generations.

In all his promises the LORD keeps faith,
he is unchanging in all his works;
the LORD holds up those who stumble
and straightens backs which are bent.
The eyes of all are lifted to thee in hope,
and thou givest them their food when it is due;
with open and bountiful hand
thou givest what they desire to every living creature.
The LORD is righteous in all his ways, unchanging in all he does;
very near is the LORD to those who call to him,
who call to him in singleness of heart.
He fulfills their desire if only they fear him;
he hears their cry and saves them.
The LORD watches over all who love him
but sends the wicked to their doom.
My tongue shall speak out the praises of the LORD,
and all thy creatures shall bless his holy name for ever and ever.

—PSALM 145:8-21 NEB

Reflection Points

1. Believing God cares about and understands every aspect of who I am—my entire physical, emotional, and spiritual makeup—helps me see why . . . .
2. When I am tired, hungry, and emotionally drained, I am more likely to experience . . . .
3. The warning signs indicating my life is veering out of balance are . . . .
4. My current daily eating patterns can best be described as . . . .
5. I am most likely to heed my need to live sensibly when . . . .
6. Hearing Jesus say, "I am the bread of life," encourages me to . . . .
7. I can tell when I have taken time to sit down quietly with the Lord and savor the good food He provides because . . . .

Additional Study

—*MEDITATE ON* Psalms 16; 34; 62; 73; 105.

—*READ ABOUT* God's life-giving provision during two mealtime scenes described in the Old and New Testaments:

Abigail, Nabal's perceptive wife and David's future bride—a multitalented desert doyenne, in 1 Samuel 25

Mary, Jesus' attentive friend from Bethany, in Luke 10:38-42.

—*STUDY* Psalm 104:14-35; Proverbs 4:20-27; Ecclesiastes 5:10-20; Matthew 4:1-4; Luke 22:7-20; Luke 24:13-35; John 21:1-14.

—*MEMORIZE* Psalm 104:14-15; Proverbs 30:8; Matthew 6:11; Matthew 7:9, 11; Luke 22:19; Philippians 4:12-13.

Suggested Exercises

- Next time you feel parched, spend a few moments studying your body's response to a glass of cool water. Notice what happens as you place the water to your lips and drink it. Write a crystal-clear description of this thirst-quenching experience. Then read and reflect on John 4:7-15 and 7:37-44.
- Pay attention to your body's hunger signals for a week and record your responses, noting how your responses to physical hunger might possibly influence, connect with, or reveal the way you respond to spiritual hunger.
- Prepare your favorite meal, or bring it home as a carry-out order. Set the table in advance with a place setting of your best dishes, flatware, stemware, and linens. Remember to bring flowers! Before you sit down, light some candles and turn off all nonessential electronic sounds—TV, radio, stereo, computer, etc. Sit down and relax, thanking the Lord as He leads you in prayer. Take time to enjoy each bite, every swallow, as you eat and drink in silence without distractions; see if you notice anything new or different. Observe what your senses tell you about your food and how you eat it, about your hunger and when it is satisfied. Spend time writing in your journal about what this experience tells you about your soul's desire to "taste and see" God's goodness.
- Monitor the mood shifts you experience over the next three days and think about how your emotions reflect any stress, hunger, fatigue, rest, or satisfaction you are feeling. How did you respond?
- Bake or buy a loaf of fresh bread. Slice off an ample piece and warm it up.

Use honey, jam, or butter, if you like. When you take the first bite, chew slowly and deliberately, as if you had never tasted fresh bread before. What do you notice?

Closing Prayer

O Thou full of compassion, I commit and commend myself unto Thee, in whom I am, and live, and know. Be Thou the Goal of my pilgrimage, and my Rest by the way. Let my soul take refuge from the crowding turmoil of worldly thoughts beneath the shadow of Thy wings; let my heart, this sea of restless waves, find peace in Thee, O God. Thou bounteous Giver of all good gifts, give to her who is weary refreshing food; gather our distracted thoughts and powers into harmony again; and set the prisoner free. See, she stands at Thy door and knocks; be it opened up to her, that she may enter with a free step, and be quickened by Thee. For Thou art the Well-spring of Life, the Light of eternal Brightness, wherein the just live who love Thee. Be it unto me according to Thy word — Amen.[9]

—AUGUSTINE OF HIPPO

For in him we live and move and have our being . . . .(Acts 17:28)

Food for Thought

Fresh bread, fresh rolls—to be formed after church, after the dough has been placed in a clean, buttered bowl to rise, covered with a clean towel during the two or more hours we are to be away at church. Sunday after Sunday, fresh rolls for lunch come steaming to the table to tempt appetites and appease hunger, as well as giving the feeling to guests of having had something especially prepared for them . . . .

We are meant to have a background for understanding what Jesus was saying when He declared in John 6:35 that He was the "bread of life" . . . . Here the Messiah, the Second Person of the Trinity, was making it known that He had come to fulfill all the promises and to be the Bread of Life Himself. What He was saying was part of the whole Word of God which was to continue to be daily bread for the spiritually hungry. When we come ~~to *the* Bread of Life,~~ Jesus Himself, we continue to be fed by "every word that proceedeth out of the mouth of the Lord" in His written Word. It is available and has been supernaturally kneaded. The ingredients needed for continued strength and help have been mixed in. It has been prepared. Long ago? Yes, but fresh every day.

Come back to Isaiah 55:2, 3: "Wherefore do ye spend money for that which is not bread? and your labour for that which satisfieth not? hearken diligently unto me, and eat ye that which is good, and let your soul delight itself in fatness. Incline your ear, and come unto me: hear, and your soul shall live . . . ."

What a beautiful way of giving us a sudden jolt! Are we in danger of spending time and money for something which is not only *not* the "bread of life," but is helping to destroy the Word of God in some way, by changing what He has blended into it in His perfect wisdom, knowledge, understanding, and love? He has prepared it for His family and the guests who are invited to "taste and see." Have we labored all our hours of one week, one month, or one year to buy material or intellectual things which will diminish our supply of true bread and the possibility of sharing it with anyone else? The warning is there, but also the urgent invitation—"eat ye that which is good." The result of this kind of eating is a delight—and, wonder of wonders, it is to be had without money and without price. Why? Because the price has already been paid for this fantastic supply of fresh bread daily, as well as the offer to come to Him who is *the* Bread of Life . . . .[10]

—EDITH SCHAEFFER, *A WAY OF SEEING*

Some Thoughts, Attitudes, Beliefs, and Behaviors That Turn People to Spiritual Junk Food

1. Depending on someone or something other than God for one's sense of identity, value, and emotional security
2. Using substitutes for love
3. Giving in when it is time to say no
4. Feeling a false sense of accomplishment, i.e., pride, when it is really by God's grace one has said no. Or yes
5. Ignoring/turning away from/neglecting/discounting God's Word
6. Worrying
7. Loving money
8. Judging others
9. Refusing to forgive
10. Being "good" in order to earn God's approval

11. Acting hypocritical
12. Feeding anger
13. Surrendering one's heart to bitterness
14. Overdoing
15. Nurturing self-pity
16. Engaging in sex (in fantasy or reality) outside marriage
17. Avoiding responsibility
18. Practicing perfectionism
19. Dishonoring parents
20. Overspending
21. Reading lots of novels, newspapers, and/or gossip/entertainment/fashion/women's/decorating/cooking magazines (*People, Us, Entertainment Weekly, Vogue, Oprah, House Beautiful, Bon Appetit*, etc.)
22. Shopping. A lot
23. Focusing on one's appearance, position, accomplishments, etc.
24. Hating someone. Anyone
25. Engaging in gossip
26. Getting drunk or high, legally or illegally
27. Overeating
28. Watching too much TV/too many movies
29. Watching TV shows and movies that increase one's appetite for spiritual junk food
30. Breaking the law, *including* the speed limit
31. Going into debt
32. Choosing criticism over kindness
33. Lying
34. Refusing to serve others
35. Smoking. Anything
36. Boasting
37. Over-controlling
38. Talking incessantly; not listening
39. Envying
40. Overworking; getting too little rest and relaxation

41. Acting cool instead of staying Christ-centered in an effort to impress, persuade, or please others
42. Gambling
43. Choosing to temporarily self-destruct
44. Using pagan, polytheistic, and/or pantheistic mind-body techniques to promote self-understanding and healing
45. Playing music all (or most of) the time
46. Over-exercising
47. Sinking into cynicism
48. Believing what the advertisers say
49. Forgetting to pray
50. Forgetting that God's love never fails

CHAPTER THREE

THE SHAPE OF OUR APPETITES: *What Satisfies Our Hunger?*

Let the humble eat and be satisfied. Let those who seek the Lord praise him and be in good heart forever.

PSALM 22:26 NEB

Beware of aspiring to a righteousness of such purity that you would not wish to be looked upon as a sinner, or, still worse, not to be one! For Christ dwells only in sinners. It was for this very reason he descended from heaven, where he had his dwelling with the righteous, to dwell among us poor sinners on earth. Meditate on love of such power, and you will then experience his consolation of love . . . . You will never find peace of mind except in Christ alone, and even then, only when you have despaired of yourself and your own works. You will also learn from him that just in the manner he has accepted you, so has he made your sins his own, and also his righteousness your own.[1]

MARTIN LUTHER (1483-1546)

True faith is coming to Jesus Christ to be saved and delivered from a sinful nature, as the Canaanite woman came to him and would not be denied. It is a faith that in love and longing and hunger and thirst and full assurance will lay hold on Christ as its loving, assured, certain and infallible Saviour.[2]

WILLIAM LAW (1686-1761)

Have you ever been sidetracked by your soul's hard-to-interpret hunger? Have you found that guiding your heart's desires demands looking directly ahead in spite of what lies around you?

Alone in her room, a college senior reads a best-selling novel recommended by a much-admired talk-show host. As soon as she finishes the final page, she writes in her journal:

> *Well, am I completely on the wrong track, or* what? *How am I going to end up feeling about teaching when I could make* a lot more *money by switching majors, going to grad school, and staying here just a few years longer? There are* so many other things I could do *that would pay* so much better!!! *I* hate *not being able to buy what I want when I go to the grocery store or the mall!!! I have this* terrible *feeling that if I don't push myself harder, I'll eventually become* frustrated *not only with my income but with* my *whole life*!! *It's still not too late to head in a different direction. So. Here's what* I really don't want:
>
> 1. I don't want *to die without feeling that I lived up to my highest potential.*
>
> 2. I don't want *to always be struggling to get by.*
>
> 3. I don't want *to miss out on having and doing things I really like.*
>
> 4. I don't want *to end up like Cassie, that poor desperate and deserted character in the book. So.* What do *I want*?

They were married forty-six years when, without any prior warning, he suffered a brain aneurysm that abruptly ended their settled life together. She was a widow at the age of seventy-one. Faith and family were invaluable sources of help. Yet as the weeks crept slowly by, she felt more and more estranged from everything and everyone around her. On a cloudy winter afternoon, she wondered: *How can I face another day without Bill? He's been gone only four months now—how can I go on without him for another five, ten, or—who knows how many more?—years, with nothing to look forward to but getting older . . . growing weaker . . . becoming a burden on all our children? Between the headaches, arthritis, money con-*

cerns, and waking up alone in our bed each morning, I don't know how much more I can take. God, what am I going to do? You know how hard this is for me, how much I still want to be with Bill. If I decide I can't continue like this, I know you'll forgive me, won't you?

A woman in her late forties volunteers in the church office for two evenings a week after her rector requests additional help. On several occasions the clergyman stays late, and the two of them begin talking about their current spiritual interests and pursuits. While standing in front of the rest-room mirror one night, she muses: *I assumed he and his wife were quite happy together, and yet he's always anxious to stay and talk. I don't know. Maybe I should leave. I don't feel entirely comfortable being here with him even though I really enjoy our discussions. I'm not sure though. Maybe I'm here for a good reason, and I should stop feeling paranoid about this. If nothing else, I could come in during the day when other people are more likely to stop by. It's usually pretty quiet around here no matter what time it is. Maybe he would appreciate my volunteering in the office no matter when I work. Maybe he would . . . .*

While leafing through the latest issue of *People*, a young mom reads an extensive article profiling several up-and-coming businesswomen. None of the women described—even those with several young children—are pictured working at home. After going to bed exhausted, she lies awake late into the night, thinking: *It seems like my life consists of nothing but facing piles of laundry and endless errand running and doing the same stuff over and over again—diaper changing,*

Through our thoughts we can be shipwrecked, and through our thoughts we can be crowned.

ANONYMOUS

Turn my heart toward your statutes and not toward selfish gain. Turn my eyes away from worthless things; preserve my life according to your word.

PSALM 119:36-37

In His will is our peace.

DANTE ALLIGHERI

toilet scrubbing, floor sweeping, pet feeding, kitchen cleanup, and everything else. When was the last time Jim seemed to notice or appreciate the things I do? I can't even remember. It seems like there's almost nothing to show for the countless hours I put in this week. This is starting to feel like a real *waste of my God-given talent and ability. Why on earth did I ever bother to get a master's degree?*

Every day each of us faces the reality of choosing where to direct our thoughts and upon whom and what we will fasten our dependence, expectations, and desires. Time after time, we're easily convinced our needs can be met, though we know our good deeds and accomplishments will steadily fade in importance, people will inevitably fail to meet our hopes and expectations, and our jobs and relationships will surely come to an end.

Following Jesus in the midst of life as it actually is requires a daily commitment to walk on His path while depending on His strength. Yielding to the authority of Christ's kingly rule and the Holy Spirit's straightforward direction is not a comfortable, automatic, or perfect process. Far from it!

"Perfect integration of feelings, thoughts, and actions is not possible in this world. It is at best a romantic dream; at worst, it is a dangerous utopian idol," author and pastor Dick Keyes observes. "The world is filled with conflict. We are called not to withdraw from it, but to be involved in it to such an extent that our sense of selfhood will sometimes be strained to the limit. Yet God is with us. His Spirit is our comforter. He not only sustains us, but gives us positive growth."[3]

In being reconciled to our personal Creator through Jesus Christ, we increasingly discover real satisfaction and freedom as we are restored to our true identity, affirms Dr. Keyes. "God's salvation restores men and women to the true image of God, the original," he says. "Our sense of identity is found first by looking to God from our innermost selves and letting all of our roles, feelings, attitudes, and relationships find themselves in relation to him."[4]

But when our sense of identity and worth become blurred, broken, or reversed—when our sense of *who we are* and *why we're valuable* is based primarily on our roles, feelings, attitudes, or relationships, rather than on God's view of us—our hearts routinely steer our soul's hunger away from God toward substitutes. Subsequently, if our dependence, expectations, and desires become focused elsewhere, our unsatisfied souls hunger for still more. Our inner appetites, fueled by an extensive array of mixed desires, beckon and then beg for relief.

To whom will we look for respite? Where will we find it?

> FOCUS POINT➢ In the secret places of our hearts we contemplate our conflicting desires and experience the ache of our hidden longings.

The polished vintage convertible idling next to my station wagon invited interest. Possibly it was the high-volume movie soundtrack pouring through my open window that drew my mind away from the stoplight overhead, made me turn my head slightly, and glance at the car's well-dressed driver. To my surprise, he was staring straight back at me. As our eyes made contact, I felt instantly embarrassed and looked away.

He noticed me, I observed, promptly checking my rearview mirror for some kind of reasonable distraction. Now what?

This time I focused on accelerating forward, with my eyes fixed straight ahead, as I clearly recalled how even considering taking a second look could break my attention on what lay before me.

I hadn't always been so determined. In years past I believed that as long as I properly redirected the energy generated by my smoldering heart, everything would remain cool. Naturally, I never had any intention of starting a real fire; I merely

We are truly indefatigable in providing for the needs of the body, but we starve the soul.

ELLEN WOOD

There are no shortcuts to any place worth going.

BEVERLY SILLS

Enjoy what you have rather than desiring what you don't have.

ECCLESIASTES 6:9 NLT

Better shun the bait than struggle in the snare.

JOHN DRYDEN

enjoyed the momentary spark, the brief energizing glow ignited inside my imagination.

It's no big deal—I can handle it, I rationalized. *No one just thinks about something and gets burned. Anyway, no one but me knows . . . .*

I didn't know then what I know now: My logic-resistant, dream-prone heart was designed for glorifying God, not for casual exposure to volatile situations. The one who made me clearly intends that my soul be minded with discreet, loving care. "Above all else, guard your heart," advises the book of Proverbs, "for it is the wellspring of life" (Prov. 4:23).

Over the years I learned that my heart holds the keys to revealing wonder and obscuring deception, transferring treasure and stockpiling venom, imparting love and absorbing evil. Within my innermost being I discovered a broad, bewildering territory that lies beyond the grasp of reason. "The heart," wrote the French mathematician and philosopher Pascal, "has its reasons which reason knows nothing of."[5]

Our hearts carry our most intimate histories—a lifetime ledger of passion and aggravation, gratitude and remorse, motives and meanings, rapture and loss. Even though God has implanted an enduring desire for eternity in our hearts, as Solomon explained in Ecclesiastes 3:11, our earthbound status urges us to satisfy our soul's hunger with mirage-like substitutes. When we do, our deepest desires remain exasperatingly unfulfilled. We cannot find soul satisfaction—and by extension, our true identity—in anything or anyone other than God.

It's easy to see how this all-too-familiar cycle starts spinning out of control: Our lingering hunger propels us toward overdoing it—over-managing, over-eating, over-thinking, over-spending, over-nurturing, over-working, over-imagining, over-ministering, over-exercising, over-estimating, over-controlling, over—you name it. Meanwhile, our appetites stimulate our unfulfilled desire for gratification. So we end up wanting more. Once our hidden cravings receive enough pseudo nourishment and random reinforcement, our desire for our favorite junk food grows more intense until, voilà, an impulsive sideways glance may unintentionally become a recurring thought pattern, which becomes a perceived need, which becomes a convincing rationale, which becomes a persistent focus, which becomes a routine habit, which becomes a fixated compulsion, which becomes an addictive dependency.

Such roadside distractions can lead to extended detours on perilous paths. It just takes one step in the wrong direction, followed by another, and then another. For proof of the various kinds of soul damage possible, we don't have to look any farther than our own hearts.

Let's be really honest about this: In the long run, it isn't just outwardly breaking one of the Ten Commandments that damages us; it's also the subtle, less startling, hunger-quelling methods we indulge in—worry, resentment, gossip, despair, discouragement, envy, conceit, doubt, scorn, vanity, deceit, ingratitude, apathy, spite, sloth, acquisitiveness, self-pity, and pride, for example. Toxic treats like these can lead us off course with heart-piercing efficiency and prevent us from seeing, knowing, and receiving God's best for us.

When considered from this vantage point, our futile attempts at alleviating our inner hunger apart from the one who creates and fills our soul's hunger seem incredibly foolish and self-destructive.

Yes, it *is* humbling to continually face the reality that Christ alone can satisfy our heart's longings and fill our soul's emptiness as we repeatedly direct our expectations, dependence, and desires elsewhere. (Admit it, we do.) But—thanks be to God!—our journey Home doesn't get cancelled whenever we lose our bearings.

Poor human reason, when it trusts in itself, substitutes the strangest absurdities for the highest divine concepts.

JOHN CHRYSOSTOM

Trust in the Lord with all your heart and lean not on your own understanding; in all your ways acknowledge him, and he will make your paths straight.

PROVERBS 3:5-6

An open door may tempt a saint.

THOMAS FULLER

FOCUS POINT➢ Jesus' invitation to follow Him ultimately calls us to be free from dependence on everything in the world apart from Him.

David's poignant words in Psalm 51 are not intended only for the "worst" sinners, but also for you and me: "The sacrifice you want is a broken spirit. A broken and repentant heart, O God, you will not despise" (Ps. 51:17 NLT). Our faithful Redeemer holds our wounded hearts in His hands even as we wander.

"The highway of holiness is not a *place*, but a way. Sanctification is not a thing to be picked up at a certain stage of our experience, and forever after possessed, but it is a life to be lived day by day, and hour by hour. We may for a moment turn aside from a path, but the path is not obliterated by our wandering, and can be instantly regained," noted Hannah Whitall Smith, the Philadelphia-born author, mother of five, and transcontinental evangelist. "And in this life and walk of faith, there may be momentary failures that, although very sad and greatly to be deplored, need not, if rightly met, disturb the attitude of the soul as to entire consecration and perfect trust, nor interrupt, for more than the passing moment, its happy communion with the Lord."[6]

As for our part in this happy communion, Mrs. Smith recommended that we never hesitate to turn toward Jesus when we fail or fall short. "The great point is an instant return to God," she asserted. "Our feeling is that it is presumptuous, and even almost impertinent, to go at once to the Lord, after having sinned against Him. It seems as if we ought to suffer the consequences of our sin first for a little while, and endure the accusings of our conscience; and we can hardly believe that the Lord *can* be willing at once to receive us back into loving relationship with Himself."[7]

That the Lord not only *can* but *is* willing to receive us may be somewhat hard for us to believe at times. But as we spend time alone with our Savior, as our souls are revived and invigorated through the heavenly nourishment of His imparted Word, the Lord graces us with the ability to "taste and see" His irresistible goodness, absolute forgiveness, and glorious love—not through someone else's expert teaching or seasoned experience, but for ourselves, first-hand! We come to understand that Jesus knows precisely the kind of mending our brokenness requires—and we learn why we can trust and rely upon God's everlasting promises. *Nothing*, the Bible tells us in Romans 8:39, *can separate us from His love*. Alleluia!

Once we accept the idea of depending on Christ to satisfy our appetites, how do we actually begin to do this? How can we increasingly know real satisfaction and fulfillment in Jesus' unfailing love for us with countless competitors for our hearts' affections?

"Desire is the throbbing pulse of human life. What we long for determines the scope of our experiences, the depth of our insights, the standards by which we judge, and the responsibility with which we choose our values," Regent College professor James Houston tells us. "Perhaps if we try to find out what our hearts truly desire, we will come to yearn for things that satisfy us better."[8]

What *do* we long for? Our desires provide powerful information about where we're heading at any particular moment and what itinerary changes may be required. Given that the distinctive shape of our appetites reflects our uniqueness, discerning our soul's vulnerabilities and identifying its chosen substitutes for Christ's spiritual food is essential. By better understanding the size and shape of our innermost appetites, we can use these built-in warning signals as reminders of our souls' ongoing need for satisfying nourishment from God.

We need not be unduly surprised, shocked, or shamed by our longings and desires this side of heaven. Instead, we can employ our spiritual hunger for God's glory. We can ask God to trans-

Honest bread is very well; it's the butter that makes the temptation.

Douglas Jerrold

Sin is first a simple suggestion, then a strong imagination, then delight, then assent.

Thomas à Kempis

Man still wishes to be happy even when he so lives as to make happiness impossible.

Augustine of Hippo

Temptation provokes me to look upward to God.

John Bunyan

form our appetites and help us satisfy them with beneficial soul food. We can turn back when we recognize we're headed in the wrong direction and instead aim the gaze of our hearts toward Jesus, the author and perfecter of our faith (Heb. 12:2)—the one and only person who can *really* fulfill our soul's deep longings.

Think of it: *Christ himself is our food, our sustenance, our life, our desire!* Knowing and believing this tremendous truth, living it out on a daily basis, marvelously transforms our nagging hunger pangs into sweet, ardent yearnings.

> FOCUS POINT➢ Soul satisfaction results from yielding to the call of Christ and the truth of God's Word, in fulfilling the purposes for which our Maker created us.

"Set your mind on things above, not on earthly things," declared the apostle Paul (Col. 3:2). Aiming to desire God above all, we can make it our daily goal to live according to the truth of our identity. As we *put on* the image of Christ, the Bible tells us we must also actively *put off* those habits, attitudes, ideas, and behaviors that sicken our souls and darken our spiritual focus (Rom. 13:12-14; Eph. 4:22-24; Col. 3:1-14).

Our growth as Christ's followers requires that we continue choosing over and over again, moment by moment, "to let go of the things that are less than God which have come to take the place of God for us," as Dr. Keyes puts it.[9] The fact that we will do this imperfectly, that we will encounter numerous failures, disappointments, heartaches, and frustrations along the way, ultimately creates a deepened awareness in us of our need for God. Needless to say, this is a *good* thing. As the Lord said to Paul: "My grace is sufficient for you, for my power is made perfect in weakness" (2 Cor. 12:9).

Yes, God's gift of grace is given freely. Certainly we can't earn it by our own effort. Without a doubt, we have done nothing whatsoever to merit God's favor. But this clearly doesn't mean that after we accept Jesus' call to follow Him, we don't play an integral part in our spiritual progress. Actually, quite the reverse is true. We do.

"Costly grace is the gospel which must be *sought* again and again, the gift which must be *asked* for, the door at which a man must *knock*," Dietrich

Bonhoeffer, the gifted German theologian and visionary twentieth-century martyr, succinctly stated. He further explained:

> Such grace is *costly* because it calls us to follow, and it is *grace* because it calls us to follow *Jesus Christ*. It is costly because it costs a man his life, and it is grace because it gives a man his only true life. It is costly because it condemns sin, and grace because it justifies the sinner. Above all it is *costly* because it cost God the life of his Son: "ye were bought at a price," and what has cost God much cannot be cheap for us. Above all, it is *grace* because God did not reckon his Son too dear a price to pay for our life, but delivered him up for us. Costly grace is the Incarnation of God.
>
> Costly grace confronts us as a gracious call to follow Jesus; it comes as a word of forgiveness to the broken spirit and the contrite heart. Grace is costly because it compels a man to submit to the yoke of Christ and follow him; it is grace because Jesus says, 'My yoke is easy and my burden is light.'"[10]

We need not shrink back in shame or collapse with chagrin at the irregularity and weakness of our hearts. Rather, when we are tempted toward discouragement, we can recall God's assurance: "The sacrifice you want is a broken spirit, a broken and repentant heart, O God, you will not despise."

As we turn back again and again and again with strenuous determination toward Jesus, our soul's sole source of sustenance and salvation, we can *ask*,

It is much easier to repent of sins we have committed than to repent of those we intend to commit.

JOSH BILLINGS

No one can live without delight, and that is why a man deprived of spiritual joy goes over to carnal pleasures.

THOMAS AQUINAS

Do not those who plot evil go astray? But those who plan what is good find love and faithfulness.

PROVERBS 14:22

seek, and *knock* to receive from Him. As we stand upon the Rock of our salvation, we hold on to God's certain promise: "If we confess our sins, he is faithful and just and will forgive us our sins and purify us from all unrighteousness" (1 John 1:9).

Again our growth in Christ requires that we choose—and keep on choosing day after day until we reach heaven "to let go of the things that are less than God which have come to take the place of God for us." By God's grace, let us respond to our appetites—not cleverly for our detriment, but wisely for our benefit—as persistent reminders of our need of God, while remembering Jesus' encouraging words: "God blesses those who realize their need for him, for the Kingdom of Heaven is given to them" (Matt. 5:3 NLT).

For the confused college senior, the disheartened widow, the exhausted mother, and the woman standing at a midlife crossroads—for all of us—the message of Jesus is the same: "Come to me, all of you who are weary and carry heavy burdens, and I will give you rest" (Matt. 11:28 NLT). He purposefully calls us away from every self-selected route to spiritual starvation. He speaks of pardon and forgiveness, of joy and rest, of good food and real satisfaction, given freely to all who depend upon Him to fill their soul's gnawing hunger.

Today Jesus bids us to receive the attentive shelteredness, indescribable beauty, and unfailing love He alone can provide. He offers to conform our identity with His own character and image as we walk with him toward heaven. He asks us to sit down with Him and enjoy His holy bounty. The question is: Will we accept or decline our King's invitation to dine at His table? Do we believe what He has said to us?

There is a path no vulture's eye hath seen,
Where lion fierce, nor lion's whelps have been,
Which leads unto that living crystal fount,
Who drinks thereof, the world doth nought account.
The depth and sea have said "'tis not in me,"
With pearl and gold it shall not valued be.
For sapphire, onyx, topaz would change;
It's hid from eyes of men, they count it strange.

Death and destruction the fame hath heard,
But where and what it is, from heaven's declared;
It brings to honour which shall ne'er decay,
It stores with wealth which time can't wear away.
It yieldeth pleasures far beyond conceit,
And truly beautifies without deceit.
Nor strength, nor wisdom, nor fresh youth shall fade,
This pearl of price, this tree of life, this spring,
Who is possessed of shall reign a king.
Nor change of state nor cares shall ever see,
But wear his crown unto eternity.
This satiates the soul, this stays the mind,
And all the rest, but vanity we find.[11]

—ANNE BRADSTREET (1612-1672),
"THE VANITY OF ALL WORLDLY THINGS"

FOCUS POINTS

➢ In the secret places of our hearts we contemplate our conflicting desires and experience the ache of our hidden longings.

➢ Jesus' invitation to follow Him ultimately calls us to be free from dependence on everything in the world apart from Him.

➢ Soul satisfaction results from yielding to the call of Christ and the truth of God's Word, in fulfilling the purposes for which our Maker created us.

NOURISHMENT FROM GOD'S WORD

Then Jesus, armed with the power of the Spirit, returned to Galilee; and reports about him spread through the whole country-side. He taught in their synagogues and all men sang his praises.

So he came to Nazareth, where he had been brought up, and went to synagogue on the Sabbath day as he regularly did. He stood up to read the lesson and was handed the scroll of the prophet Isaiah. He opened the scroll and found the passage which says,

"The spirit of the Lord is upon me because he has anointed me;
he has sent me to announce good news to the poor,
to proclaim release for prisoners and recovery of sight for the blind;
to let the broken victims go free,
to proclaim the year of the Lord's favour."

He rolled up the scroll, gave it back to the attendant, and sat down; and all eyes in the synagogue were fixed on him. He began to speak: "Today," he said, "in your very hearing this text has come true."

—LUKE 4:14-21 NEB

Jesus said to the people, "I am the light of the world. If you follow me, you won't be stumbling through the darkness, because you will have the light that leads to life."

—JOHN 8:12 NLT

Seeing that we have a great High Priest who has entered the inmost Heaven, Jesus the Son of God, let us hold firmly to our faith. For we have no superhuman High Priest to whom our weaknesses are unintelligible—he himself has shared fully in all our experience of temptation, except that he never sinned. Let us therefore approach the throne of grace with fullest confidence, that we may receive mercy for our failures and grace to help in the hour of need.

—HEBREWS 4:14-16 PHILLIPS

Unto thee, O Lord my God, I lift up my heart.
In thee I trust; do not put me to shame;
Let not my enemies exalt over me.
No man who hopes in thee is put to shame;
But shame comes to all who break faith without cause.
Make thy paths known to me, O Lord; teach me thy ways.
Lead me in thy truth and teach me; thou art God my Saviour.
For thee I have waited all the day long, for the coming of thy goodness, Lord.
Remember, LORD, thy tender care and love unfailing, shown from ages past.
Do not remember the sins and offences of my youth,
But remember me in thy unfailing love.

The Lord is good and upright;
therefore he teaches sinners in the way they should go.
He guides the humble man in doing right, He teaches the humble his ways.
All the ways of the Lord are loving and sure,
to men who keep his covenant and his charge.
For the honour of thy name, O LORD, forgive my wickedness, great as it is.
If there is any man who fears the LORD,
He shall be shown the path he should choose;
He shall enjoy lasting prosperity, and his children after him shall inherit the land.
The Lord confides his purposes to those who fear him,
and his covenant is theirs to know.
My eyes are ever on the LORD, who alone can free my feet from the net.

—PSALM 25:1-15 NEB

Reflection Points

1. When I am weary and my soul is hungry, Jesus nourishes me through . . . .
2. Maintaining my focus on what lies ahead encourages me to . . . .
3. My heart is especially vulnerable to distraction when . . . .
4. Believing that the sacrifices of God are a broken spirit and contrite heart helps me understand why . . . .
5. In linking the shape of my innermost appetites to my current situation, I see . . . .
6. Costly grace can be distinguished from cheap grace by . . . .
7. Hearing Jesus say to me, "God blesses those who realize their need of him, for the Kingdom of Heaven is given to them," changes my attitude about . . . .

Additional Study

—*MEDITATE ON* Psalms 37; 46; 51; 62; 86; 121; 130.

—*READ ABOUT* the redirected lives of these biblical women:

Rahab, Jericho's most unusual erotic entrepreneur, in Joshua 2:1-21 and 6:1-23

The *woman who "loved much"*—whose copious tears rained down upon Jesus' feet as He reclined at a Pharisee's dining table, in Luke 7:36-50

The *woman at Jacob's well*, an inquisitive Samaritan who candidly discussed water and worship with Jesus, in John 4:1-42

—*STUDY* Psalm 69:13-28; Psalm 119:25-40; Matthew 6:19-34; John 8:1-11; John 10:1-18; Romans 5:1-11; Ephesians 2:1-10; Hebrews 12:1-13.

—*MEMORIZE* Psalm 16:1-2; Psalm 32:6-7; Psalm 54:4; Psalm 62:5-6; Isaiah 55:6; Matthew 11:28-30; John 14:6; Romans 8:1-2; Gal. 5:1; 1 John 1:8-10.

Suggested Exercises

- Creating an identity diagram can provide you with a descriptive chart of your unique qualities and characteristics. It's a practical tool that can help you recognize your strengths and weaknesses, identify your appetites and desires, evaluate areas you may want to change, and reflect on your current activities, interests, and commitments. As you develop this detailed self-portrait, you may wish to use the first five categories as a starting place, plus any others you find useful. Then make a list of your past and present passions, preferences, and pursuits. Be sure to include as many names and items as you like, also noting the particular people, places, and things you dislike. Last but not least, log your time expenditures for one week. If you like, you may use the chart below as a general guide, adapting it to your needs.
- After you have completed this exercise, "draw" a word picture summarizing what you see in the identity diagram. Consider how the following Bible passages apply to what you have written: Psalm 8; Psalm 100; Psalm 139; Isaiah 43:1-2; Ephesians 2:4-10; and 1 Peter 1:3-7. Feel free to add your favorite verses in your journal as you go. When finished, store the word picture and your written diagram in a safe, convenient place where it can be easily retrieved for use during another exercise contained later in this book, as well as for your future reference. Remember, you may leave categories blank, add new headings, share this list with others, or keep it strictly private. The point is to make an identity diagram that reflects you as you are, not as you wish to be.

Identity Diagram: Who I Am Now

The characteristics I inherited:

The type of personality and temperament I possess:

The gifts and talents I believe God has given me:

The beliefs and values I have adopted as my own:
The strengths and weaknesses I have observed in myself:

The goals and aspirations I dream about:

The vision I believe God has given me for my life:

Other things worth considering:

Passions and Preferences

Extended family:

Friends:

Coworkers:

Neighbors:

Teachers:

Pastors:

Season:

Holidays:

Home activities:

Family activities:

Work activities:

Social activities:

Ministry activities:

Church activities:

Community activities:

Spiritual activities:

Creative activities:

Exercise activities:

Recreation activities:

Relaxation activities:

Self-comfort activities:

Reading spots:

Childhood memories:

Recent memories:

Toys:

Pets:

Animals:

Flowers:

Forms of art (media):

Works of art:

Books (fiction):

Books (nonfiction):

Types of music:

Piece of music:

Poems:

Jokes:

Sayings:
Stories:
Classic quotes:
Bible quotes:
Biblical characters:
Biblical events:
Bible passages:
Psalms:
Prayers:
Worship songs (contemporary):
Hymns (traditional):
Historical Figures:
Presidents:
Famous Persons:
Celebrities:
Authors (fiction):
Authors (nonfiction):
Artists:
Poets:
Musicians (instrumental):
Musicians (vocalist):
Cars:
Modes of transportation:
Stores:
Cities:
Restaurants:
Parks:
Beaches:
Vacation destinations:

Fantasies:

Escapes:

Songs:

Movies:

Magazines:

TV Shows:

Games:

Colors:

Types of food (e.g., American, Italian, Chinese):

Entrées:

Desserts:

Breads:

Vegetables:

Fruits:

Cereals:

Snacks:

Beverages:

Sounds:

Scents:

Clothing:

Fabrics:

Accessories:

Pieces of jewelry:

Cosmetic treatments:

Perfumes:

Other:

Other:

Other:

Other:

Pursuits

Books, magazines, and other reading material on my bedside table and in the bathroom:

CDs/cassette tapes in my car, computer, and/or CD/cassette players:

This month's list of video/DVD rentals and purchases:

Last five movies seen at a local theater:

Programs watched on TV during the past seventy-two hours:

My Estimated Time Expenditures This Week

For one week, keep a mental log of the amount of time you invest in your various roles, feelings, attitudes, and relationships. You may also wish to make a brief written record each evening of the estimated total time spent *per category* (two, three, four, or more areas will typically overlap). The comments and activities in parentheses are suggestions only; please feel free to adapt this list to your personal specifications in whatever way you like. At the end of the week, go through the entire list again, summarizing your comments, thoughts, insights, and reflections alongside each category heading.

Working (unpaid home-centered labor):
Working (paid labor):
Working (unpaid volunteer labor):
Ministering (if you can quantify it!):
Mothering (ditto):

Preparing food (cooking, baking, freezing, canning):

Gardening (herbs, fruits, vegetables):

Gardening (flowers):

Housecleaning:

Laundering/dry cleaning:

Sorting/organizing/putting things in their proper place:

Decorating:

Designing:

Eating at home:

Eating on the run:

Dining out:

Dieting:

Entertaining:

Dating:

Driving:

Errand running:

Traveling (work):

Traveling (leisure):

Exercising:

Taking pleasure in nature:

Enjoying and caring for pet(s):

Reading:

Writing:

Thinking:

Acting:

Reacting:

Serving:

Sleeping:

Sitting in silence:

Studying:

Relaxing:

Resting:

Praying:

Fasting:

Walking:

Hugging:

Snuggling:

Kissing:

Lovemaking:

Singing:

Shouting:

Sighing:

Laughing:

Crying:

Criticizing:

Appreciating:

Analyzing:

Observing:

Arguing:

Fighting:

Praising:

Desiring:

Giving:

Envying:

Feeling hurt:

Resenting:

Regretting:

Hoping:

Aching:

Recuperating:

Thanking:

Grieving:

Blessing:

Complaining:

Teaching:

Talking:

Dreaming:

Listening:

Repenting:

Confessing:

Worshiping:

Rejoicing:

Celebrating:

Relaxing with friends/family:

Wardrobe planning, organization, and maintenance:

Grooming (doing hair, nails, makeup at home; salon visits; consultations):

Pampering (long bath; massage; self-applied or professional spa treatments):

Computing online:

Shopping/browsing (in any form, including catalogue, online, and window):

TV watching (on-air programs):

Game playing (video, board, computer, team sports):

Movie watching (in theater):

Movie watching (at home):

Corresponding (letters, cards, E-mail):

Educational classes/associated activities:

Church/associated activities:

Arts-related activities (concerts, museum exhibitions, openings):
Community activities (organizational meetings, public speakers, forums):
Political activities (fund-raisers, rallies, lobbying, campaigning, voting):
Holidays/birthdays/special events:
Gift and food preparation related to the above:
Personal Bible study:
Set apart periods/sitting alone with God:
Hobbies:
Creative expression (art, music, textiles, pottery):
Library visits:
Gym/pool/tennis court, etc.:
Home design and decoration:
Yard maintenance and repair:
Home maintenance and repair:
Auto maintenance and repair:
Office maintenance and repair:
Financial management (paying bills, making/tracking expenditures, savings):
Emotional well-being (counseling appointments, classes, group meetings):
Physical well-being (medical appointments and treatments, classes, weight management):
Social well-being (activities with family and friends, fellowship with others, dinners, get-togethers):
Spiritual well-being (classes, group meetings, retreats, mentoring):
Other:
Other:
Other:
Other:

- Ask God often to help you recall and focus on specific phrases and verses from His Word regarding your identity in Christ. Cling to the Lord, believing what He tells you about *who He is*, *who you are,* and *where you are heading together*. Refuse to consider or accept the enemy's lies, accusations, and false advertising concerning these subjects and other related matters in the days ahead. With bright-colored markers, write down several of these Bible passages on index cards (sample formats using Philippians 3:6-8 and Hebrews 12:2-3 are shown below). Keep the cards handy for memorization and/or future reference purposes.

Eph 1-3
Ps 139

Do not be anxious about anything;
but in everything,
by prayer and petition,
with thanksgiving,
present your requests to God.
And the peace of God,
which transcends all understanding,
will guard your hearts and your minds
in Christ Jesus.
Finally . . . whatever is
. . . true,
. . . noble,
. . . right,
. . . pure,
. . . lovely,
. . . admirable:
if anything is
excellent or praiseworthy:
think about such things.

—PHILIPPIANS 4:6-8

Let us fix our eyes on Jesus,
the author and perfecter of our faith,
who for the joy set before him endured the cross,
scorning its shame,

and sat down at the right hand of God.
Consider him
who endured such opposition from sinful men,
so that you will not grow weary and lose heart.

—HEBREWS 12:2-3

Closing Prayer

Grant me, I beseech Thee, Almighty and most merciful God, fervently to desire, wisely to search out, and perfectly to fulfill all that is well-pleasing unto Thee. Order thou my worldly condition to the glory of Thy name; and, of all that Thou requirest me to do, grant me the knowledge, the desire, and the ability that I may so fulfill it as I ought, and may my path to Thee, I pray, be safe, straightforward, and perfect to the end.

Give me, O Lord, a steadfast heart, which no unworthy affection can drag downwards; give me an unconquered heart, which no tribulation can wear out; give me an upright heart, which no unworthy purpose may tempt aside.

Bestow upon me also, O Lord my God, understanding to know Thee, diligence to seek Thee, wisdom to find Thee, and a faithfulness that may finally embrace Thee. In Jesus' name, I pray. Amen.[12]

—THOMAS AQUINAS (1225-1274)

Our fears for today, our worries about tomorrow, and even the powers of hell can't keep God's love away. (Romans 8:38 NLT*)*

Food for Thought

Our love of God arises out of want, God's love to us out of fullness. Our indigence draws us to that power which can relieve, and to that goodness which can bless us. His overflowing love delights to make us partakers of the bounty he graciously imparts, not only in the gifts of his Providence, but in the richer communications of his grace. We can only be said to love God when we endeavor to glorify him, when we desire a participation of his nature, when we study to imitate his perfections.

To love God, to serve him because we love him, is therefore no less our highest happiness, than our most bounden duty. Love makes all labor light.

In some halcyon moments we are willing to persuade ourselves that religion has made an entire conquest over our heart; that we have renounced the dominion of the world, have conquered our attachment to earthly things. We flatter ourselves that nothing can now again obstruct our entire submission. But we know not what spirit we are of. We say this in the calm repose and in the stillness of the passions: when our path is smooth, our prospect smiling, danger distant, temptation absent, when we have many comforts and no trials. Suddenly, some loss, some disappointment, some privation tears off the mask, reveals us to ourselves. We at once discover that though the smaller fibers and lesser roots which fasten us down to earth may have been loosened by preceding storms, yet our substantial hold on earth is not shaken, the taproot is not cut, we are yet fast rooted to the soil, and still stronger tempests must be sent to make us let go our hold.

In our attachments to earthly things, even the most innocent, there is always the danger of excess; but from this danger we are here perfectly exempt, for there is no possibility of excess in our love to that Being who has demanded *the whole heart*. This peremptory requisition cuts off all debate. Had God required only a portion, we might be puzzled in settling the quantum. We might be plotting how large a part we might venture to keep back without absolutely forfeiting our safety; we might be haggling for deductions, bargaining for abatements, and be perpetually compromising with our Maker. But the injunction is entire, the command is definitive, the portion is unequivocal. Though it is so compressed in the expression, yet it is so expansive and ample in the measure: it is so distinct a claim, so imperative a requisition of *all* the faculties of the mind and strength, *all* the affections of the heart and soul, that there is not the least opening left for litigation—no place for anything less than absolute unreserved compliance.

Everything which relates to God is infinite. We must therefore while we keep our hearts humble, keep our aims high. Our highest services are but finite, imperfect. But as God is unlimited in goodness, he should have our unlimited love. The best we can offer is poor, but let us not withhold that best. He deserves incomparably more than we have to give. Let us not give him less than all. If he has ennobled our corrupt nature with spiritual affections, let us not refuse their noblest aspirations, to their noblest object. Let him not behold us so prodigally lavishing our affections on the meanest of his bounties, as to have nothing left for himself. As the standard of everything in religion is high, let us endeavor to act in it with the highest intention of mind, with the largest use of our faculties. Let us obey him with the most intense love, adore him with the most fervent gratitude. Let us "praise him according to his excellent greatness." Let us serve him with all the strength of our capacity, with all the devotion of our will.

Grace being a new principle added to our natural powers, as it determines the desires to a higher object, so it adds vigor to their activity. We shall best prove its dominion over us by desiring to exert ourselves in the cause of heaven with the same energy with which we once exerted ourselves in the cause of the world. The world has too little to fill our whole capacity.[13]

—HANNAH MORE (1745-1833),
PRACTICAL PIETY

CHAPTER FOUR

The Promise of a Spiritual Makeover: *Do We Really Want to Change?*

Find rest, O my soul, in God alone; my hope comes from him. He alone is my rock and my salvation; he is my fortress, I will not be shaken.

—PSALM 62:5-6

Christianity does not exist in an external conformity to practices which, though right in themselves, may be adopted from human motives and to answer secular purposes. It is not a religion of forms, modes, and decencies. It is being transformed into the image of God. It is being like-minded with Christ. It is considering Him as our sanctification as well as our redemption. It is endeavoring to live with Him here, that we might live with Him hereafter. It is desiring earnestly to surrender our will to His, our heart to the conduct of His Spirit, our life to the guidance of His word.[1]

—HANNAH MORE

Blessed is the Lord: he carries us day by day, God our salvation.

—PSALM 68:19 NEB

With a smile and a sigh, the woman sitting across from me announced, "It's *crème brûlée!* I love crème brûlée. It's absolutely my favorite dessert."

"Mine too," two more dinner partners immediately added. Around our table several people nodded in animated agreement.

Heavy cream—measured and poured into a sturdy saucepan, combined with the soft, pulpy vanilla seeds scraped from inside a split bean (please throw in the pod), and brought to the point of boiling over low heat; several large egg yolks—mixed with sugar in a heat-proof bowl until well blended, whisked over simmering water, cooked with continuous stirring until light in color and hot to the touch; pale yellow vanilla custard—well-blended cream and egg yolks placed over hot water to thicken, set in a bowl of ice water to cool, and then pushed through a strainer to improve texture (now throw out the pod). Crème brûlée—covered tightly in a bowl, chilled in the refrigerator, poured into serving dishes, sprinkled with sugar, caramelized with a blowtorch, and chilled once more before being garnished with mixed fresh berries right before serving.

Crème brûlée—so simple, so satisfying, yet so sublime—the nearly irresistible Creole concoction, a not-so-guilty pleasure enjoyed by myriad men and women who normally decline dessert. The popularity of crème brûlée is an oddity these days, for who can explain this exception to the cultural rule: "Thou shalt not eat thy entire dessert without much guilt"?

Quite often when the server brings the chef's grand finale to the table, one overhears numerous comments about the fat grams, carbs, and calories in the delicious-looking item. Or just as one is about to try a teensy sample, another attendee says, "Look at *this!* How many fat grams do you suppose it has?" Invariably someone sitting at the table knows a fairly accurate answer to this question. Therefore everyone within earshot gains even more insight on a topic millions of Americans already know a great deal about—*food*, and, more specifically, how it can make you *fat*.

So why does crème brûlée slip undetected beneath our dietary radar? With the exception of those suffering from milk allergies and other food-related ailments, thousands of banquet-goers apparently enjoy this delightful (high-fat/high-carb/high-calorie) dessert right down to the last bite, with nary a disparaging word. Truly, this is a bewildering mystery in view of the pervasive mentality associated with food, fatness, and fitness these days.

Whereas "going on a diet" was once considered an exceptional physician-prescribed measure, dieting is now an American lifestyle for nearly all of us. On any one day, an estimated 25 percent of American women are on a diet, with 50 percent finishing, breaking, or starting one.[2]

This phenomenon, of course, is not limited to women. Nearly all Americans—some say as many as 90 percent—believe they are overweight.[3] Whether discussed in terms of right and wrong ways to eat or the success or failure of specific diets, the majority of Americans seek from one meal to the next to repel the Great Enemy (spelled F-A-T).

While it's true that the percentage of overweight people has risen dramatically in recent years, and we need to aim for good health in *every* area of our lives, it's also obvious something has gone terribly wrong if our fear of weight gain becomes a dominating influence. For too many of us, our natural enjoyment of food has been twisted into an ongoing saga that never seems to quit. Today's weight-loss industry sells and promotes false dieting doctrines that misleadingly promise us everything from greater happiness and financial freedom to more satisfying and successful romantic relationships—and in the process has transformed fitness and physical attractiveness into acceptable American idols. In the Bible Christians are called to resist conforming to this kind of mold.

But we have this treasure in jars of clay to show that this all-surpassing power is from God and not from us.

2 CORINTHIANS 4:7

Give your heart to the heavenly things, not to the passing things of earth.

COLOSSIANS 3:2 PHILLIPS

A moment's insight is sometimes worth a life's experience.

OLIVER WENDELL HOLMES

"Dieting has become a religion," concludes Los Angeles psychologist Dr. Nancy Bonus. "It's no longer about health; it's about morality. If you gain weight, you're a bad person; if you lose weight, you're a good person. We have a religion-like shrine in our bathroom—the scale—and when you step on that hunk of metal, it determines your value as a person."[4]

In a candid interview with *USA Today*, Weight Watchers' founder, Jean Nidetch, confessed, "I like a cookie. Sometimes two. That's sinful for me."[5] Whereas Weight Watchers' promotion of healthy, balanced eating is a sound approach to weight management, equating eating cookies with breaking God's law is going way too far. When Nidetch proclaims, "If you can lose weight, you can do anything," from where I'm standing, at least, I can see why this striking statement isn't true.

Having bounced back and forth between losing and gaining weight countless times over twenty years, my own defenses against fat were fairly heavily fortified, reinforced by the various weight-loss regimens I'd followed. Like many others, I believed, "If I gain weight, I'm not good. To be good, I need to be thin and stay fit." My weight wasn't just a health issue for me—it was visible proof of my inner strength and personal worth.

Consequently, I became an expert on food, memorizing the caloric/carbohydrate/fat/fiber content of innumerable items, reading labels for RDAs and other nutrients, attending for-credit university classes, going to noncredit continuing education seminars and lectures, watching dozens of TV programs, buying and borrowing diet-related books, and measuring and weighing specific portion sizes. I can recite, from memory, the caloric difference between a teaspoon and tablespoon of margarine, a cup of homogenized milk and a cup of skim milk, a slice of regular whole wheat bread and a slice of "light" whole wheat bread, a medium-sized banana and a medium-sized apple. I know why it's best to order a dry potato with sour cream on the side—or, better yet, with salsa, jalapenos, and onions—instead of butter, or to eat an orange rather than drink a four-ounce glass of orange juice.

There is, of course, nothing inherently wrong with gaining such knowledge. Though when I consider the amount of time, energy, and mental focus I have invested in studying this subject, I could have earned a Ph.D. instead.

The problem was that what I ate and how much I weighed had gone beyond being a health issue for me. Food, fat, and physical attractiveness had become a determining factor of my identity.

It wasn't simply that I felt more comfortable being thinner or less healthy when I was fatter. I felt a sense of superiority and pride when I denied myself certain foods and fit into smaller-size clothes. Conversely, I felt shame and guilt when I overindulged my appetite and saw the condemning evidence of my failings reflected in our bathroom mirror. Eating was no longer about well-balanced nourishment and hunger satisfaction, discerning my appetite signals and providing basic energy for my body—it was about *who I am.*

It wasn't until I was placed in a totally uncomfortable position, where I could see things from a different vantage point, that I realized how deep the roots of my identity dependence had grown. The medical treatment of a chronic health problem required a change in my medication, prompting me to sleep and eat more than usual. Almost immediately I stopped exercising; I was too fatigued to continue leading aerobic dance classes at our church or even go for a walk. Without exercise, the debilitating pain worsened. My metabolism slowed. I began to sleep for longer periods and ate still more, without counting calories—not for one or two special meals but for every meal. By the time my doctor realized I needed a different prescription drug, it was too late. In less than six months, I had gained almost thirty pounds.

Out went my wardrobe. In came the guilt. I

My Lord and my God, take from me all that separates me from Thee! My Lord and my God, give me everything that will bring me closer to Thee! My Lord and my God, protect me from myself, and grant that I may belong entirely to Thee!

Nicholas of Flue

True religion confronts earth with heaven and brings eternity to bear upon time.

A. W. Tozer

had failed. Looking back, I suspect this is exactly where God wanted me to be, because in the dozen years that followed, I finally learned that F-A-T is not the Great Enemy after all.

> FOCUS POINT➢ This is an amazing, absolutely magnificent, almost shocking truth: At this very moment, God is conforming us to the character and image of Christ.

"Don't copy the behavior and customs of this world, but let God transform you into a new person by changing the way you think," Paul's epistle to the church in Rome advises. "Then you will know what God wants you to do, and you will know how good and pleasing and perfect his will really is" (Rom. 12:2 NLT).

I positively marvel at this verse. That God knows us through and through, accepts us as we are, and is continually teaching us about who He wants us to be and what He wants us to do is a stunning, sounds-too-good-to-be-true revelation. This is especially so when I face unexpected failure in any area of life.

When times of testing, trouble, trial, and temptation come, as Christians we may wonder how God could possibly be at work within us "to will and to act according to his good purpose" (Phil. 2:13). But His Word assures us that *He is actively at work within us*. We experience many types of pain, heartache, and frustration along the road, causing us to sometimes question what God is doing, but *He has already told us what He is doing* (e.g., Rom. 8:28; 2 Cor. 3:18; Heb. 10:16; 1 Pet. 1:3-5). We may never know the exact whys and whens and hows of His plans for us, but we can rest in the assurance that *He has always known His plans for us* (e.g., Ps. 33:11; Jer. 29:11-13 and 32:38-41; John 3:16; Eph. 1:4-12; Col. 1:22).

It's sometimes easy to "misplace" these marvelous truths as we negotiate the unpredictable flow of our stressful lives. Perhaps we forget them because yielding our bodies, minds, and souls to Christ is not a once-and-for-all commitment. It's a moment-by-moment walk, often characterized by two steps forward and one step back. Learning what it means to belong to God as we become more like His Son requires genuine humility and patience. We receive invaluable lessons, not only through our triumphs but also from our failures.

In an age of instant online access and store-bought solutions, we feel frustrated when we're reminded that our soul's transformation is an ongoing, lifelong, mysterious process.

God sees our hearts; He knows our thoughts. Wherever we go, whatever we do, He is with us. Our Creator perceives our thoughts from afar and is familiar with *all* our ways, even to the extent of knowing each word before we speak it. "Such knowledge is too wonderful for me," pondered David, "too lofty for me to attain" (Ps. 139:1-6).

It's not as though our sovereign Creator puts on a pair of rose-colored glasses to mask our innumerable flaws as He watches over us. The Bible tells us: "The LORD does not look at the things man looks at. Man looks at the outward appearance, but the LORD looks at the heart" (1 Sam. 16:7). Our heavenly Father wants us to *see* and *know* His divine purposes for us as we cooperate with the Holy Spirit's unfaltering work within us.

When we become Christians, we may or may not *feel* different about ourselves. We may not remember the exact moment of our conversion or fully appreciate the circumstances surrounding it or pinpoint when we knew by faith that Jesus is who He said He is. No matter what we felt then or what we remember, appreciate, or comprehend about it now, a number of permanent changes and supernatural events occurred inside us, and also in heaven, when we came to know Jesus as our Lord and Savior.

At the time of our conversion, we acquired a brand-new status in the kingdom of God—we

To deny self is to become a nonconformist. The Bible tells us not to be conformed to this world either physically or intellectually or spiritually.

BILLY GRAHAM

I am most joyously content that Christ would break all my idols to bits. It renews my love for Christ to see that He is jealous of my love, and will have it all to Himself.

SAMUEL RUTHERFORD

were "made right in God's sight by faith," or justified. We now "have peace with God because of what Jesus Christ our Lord has done for us" (Rom. 5:1 NLT). The blood Christ shed on the cross has cleansed us from our sins and given us eternal life. God subsequently looks upon us as though we are perfectly righteous, as though we had never sinned and will never sin again, based on the perfect righteousness of Christ provided us by God's love, mercy, and grace.

Our justification through faith and our peace with God through Christ "brought us into this place of highest privilege where we now stand" (Rom. 5:2 NLT)—the divinely protected place made possible by God's incomparable grace. We stand where we are today because of this enduring event, a once-and-for-all-time action on God's part. Nothing we do can change, destroy, alter, or reverse what the Lord has already accomplished for us.

"To those who are Christ's," says author and theologian J. I. Packer, "the holy God is a loving Father; they belong to His family; they may approach Him without fear, and always be sure of His fatherly concern and care. This is the heart of the New Testament message."[6]

Our heavenly Father's love for us, the way He relates to us, the promised provision of His mercy, do not change when we fail to live up to His expectations. Our efforts to earn or return His love do not determine the quality of the permanent Father-daughter relationship we are privileged to share with Him. The Bible tells us this relationship was first made possible through the perfect righteousness we receive from His Son by faith, rather than through any imperfect righteousness of our own.

Another permanent life-changing event that took place upon our conversion happened when God "made us alive with Christ" (Eph. 2:5). This new birth, or *regeneration*, occurred inside us when we became Christians. When our mother and father conceived us and gave us temporary, natural, biological life, they became *in reality* our genetic parents. Likewise, when God gave us eternal, supernatural, nonbiological life on the day of our spiritual rebirth, He became *in reality* our heavenly Father.

"You are a child of God in a *literal*, not a metaphorical sense," physician Dr. John White explains. "But the life must grow and develop. As it does so, you will reflect, more and more, the likeness of the Father from whom the life came, just as some degree of likeness to your physical parents accompanies growth in your physical and emotional life."[7] Dr. White further notes:

> As God's life within you grows, it will influence both your emotional and your physical development. You will become more mature emotionally. Other things being equal, you will enjoy better physical health. Your new birth does not guarantee that you will never be emotionally or physically sick, but it will move you in the direction of improved health.
>
> For your new life to grow, it must be fed and exercised. The food it requires is the Holy Scriptures. Exercise will consist of obedience by faith to the commands of God. You will also need to breathe deep drafts of heavenly air as your prayer life develops.
>
> Once alienated from God, you have changed to being at peace with him as well as being his child. Christ, his unique Son whom you may have formerly ignored, now has a relationship with you which is many-faceted. He is your Shepherd and you are his sheep . . . . He is the bread on whom you feed. He is the light illuminating your interior darkness. And so we could go on. What in essence all of this means is that you now belong to him and he to you in a relationship of vital interchanges. Bonds have been established between you that nothing in heaven, earth, or hell can break.[8]

In him we have redemption through his blood, the forgiveness of sins, in accordance with the riches of God's grace that he lavished on us with all wisdom and understanding.

EPHESIANS 1:7

Our peace with God is not just some introspective thing. It is a peace based upon God's promise that Christ's atoning death is enough to meet all our present failures.

FRANCIS SCHAEFFER

Through God's divinely directed process, our Maker creates our new identity in the character and image of His Son, in order that we may be set free from sin and that Christ's life may be expressed through us. About this experience the apostle Paul wrote: "Now the Lord is the Spirit, and where the Spirit of the Lord is, there is freedom. And we, who with unveiled faces all reflect the Lord's glory, are being transformed into his likeness with ever-increasing glory, which comes from the LORD, who is the Spirit" (2 Cor. 3:17-18).

This is an unfathomable paradox: By responding to our heavenly Father's unfailing love for us, obeying His commands, and yielding to His tender care, we become more like Jesus—and discover who *we really* are.

> FOCUS POINT➢ As we give our lives and hearts more fully to Christ, we "come to ourselves," with a deepening sense of who God has created us to be and who we are becoming.

Knowing in our heads about God's promise of a spiritual makeover is one thing, while hungering and thirsting for it with our whole hearts is quite another. The central question is, do we really *want* to change?

Because our self-image is deeply impacted by the society in which we live, it's necessary for us to stand back and examine the culture and then consciously commit ourselves day by day to making a change as we keep asking God to transform our desires according to His will. Our idols, after all, don't need to be carved in stone to attract our attention; they come in a colorful variety of attractive shapes and forms, whether we recognize them or not. If Christ is to be Lord of our hearts, He must also become ruler of our appetites.

Think for a moment of a food you always avoid eating because you can't stand its taste, smell, or texture. Perhaps you once developed food poisoning after eating it, or you may have disagreeable associations with its consumption. As a result, the thought or smell of this food provokes strong feelings of disgust, repulsion, or even nausea. More than likely, your closest friends and family members can name the particular food you can't or won't eat.

One of the Holy Spirit's most helpful gifts to us is the inward disgust, repulsion, or loathing our souls experience when He convicts us of some specific sin. If we willingly place our appetites on God's altar, praying, "Your will be done," we will be changed in ways we never imagined. We become brand-new women with entirely new dreams and desires. If we increasingly aim our hunger toward Christ and His kingdom, crying, "Have mercy on me, O God, according to your unfailing love," the Holy Spirit will transform our appetites as He remakes our minds and reshapes our thinking about the world we live in. We will acquire a taste for grace.

"A person has to get fed up with the ways of the world before he, before she, acquires an appetite for the world of grace," acknowledges pastor Eugene H. Peterson. "The first step toward God is a step away from the lies of the world. It is a renunciation of the lies we have been told about ourselves and our neighbors and our universe."[9]

Repentance is "the usual biblical word describing the no we say to the world's lies and the yes we say to God's truth. It is always and everywhere the first word in the Christian life," observes Dr. Peterson, adding:

> Repentance is not an emotion. It is not feeling sorry for your sins. It is a decision. It is deciding that you have been wrong in supposing that you could manage your own life and be your own god; it is deciding that you were wrong in thinking you had, or could get, the strength, education and training to make it on your own; it is deciding you have been told a pack of lies about yourself and your neighbor and your world. And it is deciding that God in Jesus Christ is telling you the truth. Repentance is a realization that

A God who let us prove his existence would be an idol.

DIETRICH BONHOEFFER

The "world" means the organization and the mind and the outlook of mankind as it ignores God.

MARTYN LLOYD-JONES

I tell you the truth, whoever hears my word and believes him who sent me has eternal life and will not be condemned; he has crossed over from death to life.

JOHN 5:24

> what God wants from you and what you want from God are not going to be achieved by doing the same old things, thinking the same old thoughts. Repentance is a decision to follow Jesus Christ and become his pilgrim in the path of peace.[10]

Through Christ we are offered real freedom from the world's lies as we acquire new appetites and say yes to God's truth. As our hunger is drawn toward God's kingdom and our minds are set on Christ and His Word, we are guarded from Satan's deceit. Our transformed desires become a vital source of protection. With God's help, we increasingly discover how our identities have been culturally molded and learn how to change through comprehensive Bible study; the infilling, intercession, and guidance of the Holy Spirit; private prayer and quiet reflection; the counsel and mentoring we receive from mature believers; our obedience by faith to God's commands; and an ongoing reciprocal relationship with the Christians with whom we regularly meet for worship, prayer, ministry, and teaching.

When we give ourselves up to Christ's lordship, our identity is still affected by, among other things, our family, peer group, social status, ethnicity, local community, nationality, and global position, but our self-concept is no longer controlled or principally influenced by the world. Our Father in heaven is in charge of shaping our character and identity now.

Thank God for the grace of repentance—His liberating gift of life that results in our *turning away* from the things of this world and *turning toward* our Savior and Lord, Jesus Christ. Living *in* the world does not mean we are designed to be *of* it! The following passage illuminates one of the reasons why:

> *For we died and were buried with Christ by baptism. And just as Christ was raised from the dead by the glorious power of the Father, now we also may live new lives. Since we have been united with him in his death, we will also be raised as he was. Our old sinful selves were crucified with Christ so that sin might lose its power in our lives. We are no longer slaves to sin. For when we died with Christ we were set free from the power of sin. And since we died with Christ, we know we will also share his new life . . . . give yourselves*

completely to God since you have been given new life." (Rom. 6:4-8, 13 NLT)

Dead . . . buried . . . and back to life again. Dead to sin but alive to God! *Turning away* from our old way of living and thinking and being, from all that would hold us back from walking with Jesus in freedom and truth. *Turning toward* our souls' true satisfaction—our heart's desire, Jesus Christ—as we walk with our Savior and Lord in newness of life by faith. Here lies the true secret of our contentment.

"Jesus Christ lives indeed in the presence of the Father. This is where we are called to live. We are to be dead in the present life! Dead both to good and bad, in order to be alive in the presence of God. This is what it means to love God enough to be contented; to love him enough in this present world to say, 'Thank you' in all the ebb and flow of life," clarified the twentieth-century theologian Francis Schaeffer. "When I am dead to both good and bad, I have my face turned toward God. I am then the creature in the presence of the Creator, acknowledging that he is my Creator, and I am only a creature, nothing more. It is as though I am already in the grave, and already before the face of God."

Dr. Schaeffer also said something more: "But one more note needs to be sounded. We must not stop here! When through faith I am dead to all, and am face to face with God, than I am ready by faith to *come back into this present world*, as though I have been raised from the dead. It is as though I anticipate that day when I *will* come back."[11]

You can't tell the exact moment when night becomes day, but you know when it is daytime.

ANONYMOUS

All adventures, especially into new territory, are scary.

SALLY RIDE

The kingdom of heaven is like treasure hidden in a field. When a man found it, he hid it again, and then in his joy went and sold all he had and bought that field.

MATTHEW 13:44

Christ's finished work on the cross has provided for our permanent personal transformation, a head-to-toe spiritual makeover that will last for eternity, the complete restoration of our bodies, minds, and souls. Through this glorious, ongoing, deliberate work of God's sanctification, He is not only making us whole—He is making us holy.

Jesus said to His disciples, "If any of you wants to be my follower, you must put aside your selfish ambition, shoulder your cross, and follow me. If you try to keep your life for yourself, you will lose it. But if you give up your life for me, you will find true life. And how do you benefit if you gain the whole world but lose your own soul in the process? Is anything worth more than your soul?" (Matt. 16:24-26 NLT).

No wonder we get so confused! The nonstop rhythm that many of us—my family, my friends, I, and perhaps you—seem to effortlessly glide into demands assessment. The predominant perspective of our culture, the message we hear repeated *ad infinitum* everywhere around us is that if we hope to be of real "value," we must strive for success—fight fat, work to win, find a mate, wow the boss, mother model kids, acquire the best, dress to impress—in a continuing effort to be someone or achieve something of "worth." Clearly, this is not what Jesus said about where our enduring worth resides.

> FOCUS POINT➢ Through everything we encounter on our way Home, we need to continually keep God's design for us in mind.

"The kingdom of God," Prison Fellowship founder Charles Colson reminds us, "is a kingdom of paradox, where through the ugly defeat of the cross a holy God is utterly glorified. Victory comes through defeat; healing through brokenness; finding self through losing self."[12]

From a biblical point of view, the bent of our culture—the things of this world—stand in direct opposition to the kingdom of heaven. As Christians, the reason for our success is this: "*Christ in you, the hope of a glory to come*" (Col. 1:27 NEB). So, if we are fighting to win, on whose side are we fighting? Upon whom and what does our identity depend? Upon what source of sustenance, guidance, and truth do we rely?

There are zero shortcuts on the path of discipleship. Our inner transformation isn't simply skin deep—a quick-change cosmetic feat intended to make us look good. Though looks definitely count a great deal in our ephemeral environment, in the kingdom of heaven where we permanently reside, it's a different story.

"What we love we shall grow to resemble," said the wise monk Bernard of Clairvaux in the twelfth century. That principle still applies today: Our *values* directly shape our *identity*. As women created in God's image, we have been uniquely endowed with the ability to externally portray what we internally treasure. Thus, there is no avoiding the direct link between what and whom we value and how we think and act. Our beliefs powerfully affect our behavior; our heart's innermost attitudes surface in outward actions. *What we love we shall grow to resemble.* This is true of no other creature on earth.

Consider, for example, how your total appearance—your weight, clothing, hairstyle, mannerisms, facial expressions, posture, and body language—has been shaped by what you value. Who are your role models? Whose opinions have most influenced the image you hope to present to others?

The Lord loves, redeems, and sanctifies us individually with an *everlasting* love. Our physical appearance is not what makes us beautiful in His sight: "Your beauty should reside, not in outward adornment—the braiding of the hair, or jewelry, or dress—but in the inmost center of your being,

Christ is the only way to God, but there are as many ways to Christ as there are people who come to Him.

Os Guinness

Courage is almost a contradiction in terms. It means a strong desire to live taking the form of a readiness to die.

G. K. Chesterton

When Christ calls a man, He bids him come and die.

Dietrich Bonhoeffer

with its imperishable ornament, a gentle, quiet spirit, which is of high value in the sight of God" (1 Pet. 3:3-4 NEB).

Isn't this an encouraging antidote to the messages about physical attractiveness we constantly receive from today's culture? By focusing our heart's desires on Christ and letting the Holy Spirit transform us from the inside out, we are indeed becoming beautiful where it really counts.

Are we willing to let go of our ideas about what our makeovers should "look" like and give God permission to reshape us according to His perfect will for us, not only regarding our physical appearance but in every area of our lives? To remove from us the undesirable appetites that diminish our hunger for God's holiness? To replace our distracting cravings with single-minded yearning for the Bread of Life?

"Am I prepared to let God grip me by His power and do a work in me that is worthy of Himself?" asked missionary and evangelist Oswald Chambers. "Sanctification is not my idea of what I want God to do for me; sanctification is God's idea of what He wants to do for me, and He has to get me into the attitude of mind and spirit where at any cost I will let Him sanctify me wholly."[13]

Day by day we can choose to turn away from the appealing ambitions and dead-end desires that drive us to substitutes. Moment by moment we can ask Jesus to strengthen and sustain us by His Comforter and Counselor, the Holy Spirit, as we look forward to meeting our beloved Savior face to face. Though our heavenward journey is painfully rugged, what a life-changing difference it makes knowing our Savior is with us every step of the way. Jesus, the author and finisher of our faith, goes before and behind us; He asks us to do nothing that He did not first show us how to do through His own witness and example, as one of us.

"Our blessed Redeemer, in overcoming the world, bequeathed us his command to overcome it also, but as he did not give the command without the example, so he did not give the example without the offer of a power to obey the command," affirmed eighteenth-century author and abolitionist Hannah More.[14]

We can wholeheartedly trust God to "carry us day by day," remembering that His Son is the living source of our soul's sustenance on our way Home. As real battles and hard choices invite us to surrender our lives more fully to Christ, our marvelous remaking is creating an inner radiance time cannot erase, allowing us to become forever beautiful in our Lord's sight. What's more, shouldn't His opinion far outweigh everyone else's?

I had been hungry, all the Years—
My Noon had Come—to dine—
I trembling drew the Table near—
And touched the Curious Wine—

'Twas this on Tables I had seen—
When turning, hungry, Home.
I looked in Windows, for the Wealth
I could not hope—for Mine—

I did not know the ample Bread—
'Twas so unlike the Crumb
The Birds and I had often shared
In Nature's—Dining Room—

The Plenty hurt me—'twas so new—
Myself felt ill—and odd—
As Berry of a Mountain Bush—
Transplanted—to the Road—

Nor was I hungry—so I found—
That Hunger—was a way
Of Persons outside Windows—
The Entering—takes away.[15]

—EMILY DICKINSON
(1830-1886)

The important thing isn't saying the right words but, perhaps for the first time in your life, talking heart to heart with God and inviting Him in.

LUIS PALAU

Christian spirituality does not begin with us talking about our experience; it begins with listening to God call us, heal us, forgive us.

EUGENE H. PETERSON

How goodness heightens beauty!

HANNAH MORE

Focus Points

➢ This is an amazing, absolutely magnificent, almost shocking truth: At this very moment, God is conforming us to the character and image of Christ.

➢ Through everything we encounter, we need to continually keep God's design for us in mind.

➢ As we give our lives and hearts more fully to Christ, we "come to ourselves," with a deepening sense of who God has created us to be and who we are becoming.

Nourishment from God's Word

I am the real vine and my Father is the gardener. Every barren branch of mine he cuts away; and every fruiting branch he cleans, to make it more fruitful still. You have already been cleansed by the word that I spoke to you. Dwell in me, as I in you. No branch can bear fruit by itself, but only if it remains united with the vine; no more can you bear fruit, unless you remain united with me. . . .

If you dwell in me, and my words dwell in you, ask what you will, and you shall have it. This is my Father's glory, that you may bear fruit in plenty and so be my disciples. As the Father has loved me, so I have loved you. Dwell in my love. If you heed my commands, you will dwell in my love, as I have heeded my Father's commands and dwell in his love.

I have spoken thus to you, so that my joy may be in you, and your joy complete. This is my commandment: love one another, as I have loved you. There is no greater love than this, that a man should lay down his life for his friends. You are my friends, if you do what I command you. I call you servants no longer; a servant does not know what his master is about. I have called you friends, because I have disclosed to you everything that I have heard from my Father. You did not choose me: I chose you. I appointed you to go on and bear fruit, fruit that shall last; so that the Father may give you all that you ask in my name. This is my commandment to you: love one another.

—JOHN 15:1-4, 7-17 NEB

And we know that in all things God works for the good of those who love him, who have been called according to his purpose. For those God foreknew he also predestined to be conformed to the likeness of his Son, that he might be the first-

born among many brothers. And those he predestined, he also called; those he called, he also justified; those he justified, he also glorified.

What, then, shall we say in response to this? If God is for us, who can be against us? He who did not spare his own Son, but gave him up for us all—how will he not also, along with him, graciously give us all things? Who will bring any charge against those whom God has chosen? It is God who justifies. Who is he that condemns? Christ Jesus, who died—more than that, who was raised to life—is at the right hand of God and is also interceding for us. Who shall separate us from the love of Christ? Shall trouble or hardship or persecution or famine or nakedness or danger or sword? As it is written:

> *"For your sake we face death all day long;*
> *We are considered as sheep to be slaughtered." [Ps. 44:22]*

No, in all these things we are more than conquerors through him who loved us. For I am convinced that neither death nor life, neither angels nor demons, neither the present nor the future, nor any powers, neither height nor depth, nor anything else in all creation, will be able to separate us from the love of God that is in Christ Jesus our Lord.

—ROMANS 8:28-39

> *The Spirit of the Sovereign LORD is on me,*
> *because the LORD has anointed me to preach good news to the poor.*
> *He has sent me to bind up the brokenhearted,*
> *to proclaim freedom for the captives*
> *and release from darkness for the prisoners,*
> *to proclaim the year of the LORD's favor*
> *and the day of vengeance of our God, to comfort all who mourn,*
> *and provide for those who grieve in Zion—*
> *to bestow on them a crown of beauty instead of ashes,*
> *the oil of gladness instead of mourning,*
> *and a garment of praise instead of a spirit of despair.*
> *They will be called oaks of righteousness,*
> *a planting of the LORD for the display of his splendor. . . .*
> *I delight greatly in the LORD; my soul rejoices in my God.*

For he has clothed me with garments of salvation
and arrayed me in a robe of righteousness,
as a bridegroom adorns his head like a priest,
and as a bride adorns herself with her jewels.
For as the soil makes the sprout come up
and a garden causes seeds to grow,
so the Sovereign LORD will make righteousness and praise
spring up before all nations.

—ISAIAH 61:1-3, 10-11

REFLECTION POINTS

1. Knowing the Lord is divinely directing my spiritual makeover helps me understand why . . . .
2. Basing my self-worth on how I look or what I achieve seems . . . .
3. When I lack self-control or know I have sinned, repentance provides . . . .
4. Inner beauty is developed by . . . .
5. Letting God transform me into a new person by changing the way I think has required . . . .
6. Heart attitudes have a powerful impact on external appearances because . . . .
7. For me, single-minded devotion to Christ means . . . .

ADDITIONAL STUDY

—*MEDITATE ON* Psalms 4; 25; 32; 40; 51; 103; 116.

—*READ ABOUT* these New Testament women who received life-changing spiritual makeovers through faith in Jesus Christ:

Mary of Magdala, Jesus' devoted follower on the road, near the cross, and at the tomb, in Luke 8:1-3; 23:49—24:11; John 19:25; 20:1-18. (See also Matt. 27:55—28:10; Mark 15:40—16:11).

The *Syrophoenician Woman*, whose persistent faith risked Jesus' rebuke, Mark 7:24-30.

Damaris, one of two seekers converted at a prestigious Athenian philosophy center, in Acts 17:16-34.

—*STUDY* Proverbs 2:1-11; John 3:1-21; John 14:15-21; Romans 8:1-17; Ephesians 2:1-10; Colossians 3:1-17; Titus 2:11-14; 3:3-8; 1 John 2:15-17.

—*MEMORIZE* Psalm 27:1-2, 4-5; Psalm 139:23-24; John 6:63; John 14:27; Romans 12:1-2; 2 Corinthians 3:17-18; 5:17; and Colossians 1:27.

Suggested Exercises

- According to Jesus, what impact does "gaining the whole world" have upon the soul (Matt. 16:24-26). Explain what this loss means—and how it happens—in your own words.
- In his writings Bernard of Clairvaux vividly described his soul's hunger for God and the rich satisfaction he found in loving Christ. After reading the following passage, reflect on your own experience of "the renewal and remaking" of the spirit of your mind. As you look back over the time you have known and walked with Christ, how have your appetites, longings, and desires changed? In what ways does Jesus fill, encourage, direct, and strengthen your heart? Record your answers, thoughts, and prayers in your journal.

> If you ask me how I know that the Lord is present, since His ways are past finding out, my answer is that the Word is living and active, and as soon as He entered me, He aroused my sleeping soul, and stirred and softened and pricked my heart that had been sick and as hard as stone.
>
> He began to pluck up and destroy, to build and plant, to water the dry places and shed light upon the dark, to open what was shut, to warm the chill, to make the crooked straight and the rough places plain; so that my soul has blessed the Lord and all that is within me has praised His holy Name.
>
> Thus has the Bridegroom entered into me; my senses told me nothing of His coming; I knew that He was present only by the movement of my heart. I perceived His power, because it put my sins to flight and exercised a strong control on all my impulses. I am moved to wonder at His wisdom too, uncovering my secret faults and teaching me to see their sinfulness; and I have experienced His gentleness and kindness in such measure as to astonish me.

> In the renewal and remaking of the spirit of my mind—that is, my inmost being—I have beheld the beauty of His glory and have been filled with awe as I gazed at His manifold greatness.[16]

- Read 2 Peter 1:3-11 NIV, and then fill in the blanks below. Save this list as an encouraging reminder to keep aiming your heart toward heaven on both easy and difficult days.

God's divine power has given me______________________________

through my knowledge of__________________________________.

He has given me____

so that through them I may____________________________________

____.

For this reason, I am to make every effort to ____________________

____

____

______________________________________.

For if I possess these qualities in increasing measure, they will

____.

But if I do not have them, I am ____________________________

____.

Therefore,____

__________________________________.

For if I do these things, I will _____________________________________

____

____.

- Pastor and author A. W. Tozer (1897-1963) once wrote that people can be known by what they think about most, what they desire most, how they use their money and their leisure time, what they laugh at, who and what they admire, and by the company they keep. Given what you know about Christ's life from reading the Bible, describe what you have learned from His example and teaching concerning the following areas:

Thoughts:

Desires:

Use of money:

Use of leisure time:

Things laughed at:

Whom and what admired:

Company kept:

- Using the identity diagram you completed for chapter 3, how is your identity currently reflected in these areas?

Thoughts:

Desires:

Use of money:

Use of leisure time:

Things laughed at:

Whom and what admired:

Company kept:

- In what ways, if any, might the Holy Spirit be prompting you to move in a new direction regarding these areas of your life?

Thoughts:

Desires:

Use of money:

Use of leisure time:

Things laughed at:

Whom and what admired:

Company kept:

Closing Prayer

We love Thee, O our God; and we desire to love Thee more and more. Grant to us that we may love Thee as much as we desire, and as much as we ought. O dearest Friend, who hast so loved and saved us, the thought of whom is so sweet and always growing sweeter, come with Christ and dwell in our hearts; then Thou wilt keep a watch over our lips, our steps, our deeds, and we shall not need to be anxious either for our souls or our bodies. Give us love, sweetest of all gifts, which knows no enemy. Give us in our hearts pure love, born of Thy love to us, that we may love others as Thou lovest us. O most loving Father of Jesus Christ, from whom floweth all love, let our hearts, frozen in sin, cold to Thee and cold to others, be warmed by this divine fire. So help and bless us in Thy Son—Amen.[17]

—ANSELM OF CANTERBURY
(1033-1109)

> *For we are God's masterpiece. He has created us anew in Christ Jesus, so that we can do the good things he planned for us long ago. (Ephesians 2:10 NLT)*

Food for Thought

Until you have given up your real self to Him, you will not have a real self. Sameness is to be found most among the most "natural" men, not among those who surrender to Christ. How monotonously alike all the great tyrants and conquerors have been: how gloriously different are the saints.

But there must be a real giving up of the self. You must throw it away "blindly" so to speak. Christ will indeed give you a real personality, but you must not go to Him for the sake of that. As long as your own personality is what you are bothering about, you are not going to Him at all. The very first step is to try to forget about the self altogether. Your real, new self (which is Christ's and also yours, and yours just because it is His) will not come as long as you are looking for it. It will come when you are looking for Him. Does that sound strange?

The same principle holds, you know, for more everyday matters. Even in social life, you will never make a good impression on other people until you stop thinking about what sort of impression you are making. Even in literature and art, no man who bothers about originality will ever be original: whereas if you simply try to tell the truth (without caring twopence how often it has been told before), you will, nine times out of ten, become original without ever having noticed it.

The principle runs through all life from top to bottom. Give up yourself, and you will find your real self. Lose your life and you will save it. Submit to death, death of your ambitions and favourite wishes every day and death of your whole body in the end: submit with every fibre of your being, and you will find eternal life. Keep back nothing. Nothing that you have not given away will ever be really yours. Nothing in you that has not died will ever be raised from the dead. Look for yourself, and you will find in the long run only hatred, loneliness, despair, rage, ruin, and decay. But look for Christ, and you will find Him, and with Him everything else thrown in.[18]

—C. S. LEWIS
(1898-1963)

CHAPTER FIVE

The Joy and Passion of Waiting on God:

Where Can We Find Good Nourishment?

Turn to the LORD, your strength; seek his presence always.

—PSALM 105:4 NEB

Salvation is not merely deliverance from sin, nor the experience of personal holiness; the salvation of God is deliverance out of self entirely into union with Himself. My experimental knowledge of salvation will be along the line of deliverance from sin and of personal holiness; but salvation means the spirit of God has brought me into touch with God's personality, and I am thrilled with something infinitely greater than myself; I am caught up into the abandonment of God.[1]

—OSWALD CHAMBERS

Whom have I in heaven but you? And earth has nothing I desire besides you. My flesh and my heart may fail, but God is the strength of my heart and my portion forever.

—PSALM 73:25-26

When Christ bids us to walk with Him in newness of life, He invites us to leave behind an identity wrapped up in things that won't last. There's no mistaking His intention.

As Christians, we find our identity in something beyond ourselves. By faith we believe that our Father is forming our character and identity in the image of His Son as we surrender our lives to the remaking. Waiting upon Christ in His Word helps build our identity from God's point of view.

"If you are a Christian, your final environment is a world whose Creator forgives, accepts, and loves you in all your uniqueness," Dick Keyes reminds us. "God not only loves you this way, but he wants you to always be aware of it. He wants you to have that confidence and to live in it."[2]

Shame often comes to us disguised as humility, but the fruit shame produces in our lives betrays its capacity for devastation. Depression, suicidal thoughts, self-hatred, eating disorders (including anorexia, bulimia, constant dieting, and obesity), viewing oneself as a victim, and personal neglect are all rooted in shame. Women are particularly vulnerable to these emotional disorders—even those who have been redeemed and forgiven by Jesus Christ. Why? Is this really the way God wants women to live?

Just as the Bible teaches us to avoid placing our self-worth in our abilities and accomplishments, it also teaches us to avoid the other extreme—that is, seeing ourselves as worthless, incompetent, and unlovable. Like those who were the "first fruits" of the early church, we too can marvel at what it means to be born into the kingdom of God and be "brand-new" through Christ. "Every good and perfect gift is from above, coming down from the Father of the heavenly lights, who does not change like shifting shadows. He chose to give us birth through the word of truth, that we might be a kind of first fruits of all he created" (James 1:17-18). Then, as we increasingly appreciate the extent of God's love for us, we will grow in our ability to receive and use God's good gifts. We will learn why shame—a destructive emotion that combines feelings of humiliation, dishonor, unworthiness, and disgrace—is altogether incompatible with the kind of self-acceptance that rests on God's unfailing love for His cherished children. Dr. Keyes states:

> I do not accept myself just because it is easier, the psychologically healthy thing to do, or because everybody else says it's a good idea. I can accept myself because God has forgiven and accepted me, because he loves me and wants to spend time with me. This is my basis of personal value and worth.
>
> In crude terms of economics, a thing is worth what someone is willing to pay for it. In the cross of Jesus Christ, we have a full picture of what God was willing to give for the life of the Christian. There is no higher mark of value imaginable. Self-acceptance is built on the growing understanding and appreciation of the forgiveness and acceptance of God.[3]

For women living in a world where self-worth is measured in dollars and ounces, in professional credentials and daily inventories, these words bring a sweet sense of relief.

How do we become more aware of God's forgiveness, acceptance, and love for us in all our uniqueness? In what ways does our confidence in God's love for us grow? If we want our self-acceptance to become deeply rooted in Christ, how do we build our understanding of God's love, grace, and forgiveness?

"Grow in grace and understanding of our Master and Savior, Jesus Christ," encouraged the apostle Peter. "Glory to the Master, now and forever! Yes!" (2 Peter 3:18 THE MESSAGE). Our growth in grace and understanding of our Master and Savior requires patient waiting on Jesus Christ

Yet the Lord longs to be gracious to you; he rises to show you compassion. For the Lord is a God of justice. Blessed are all who wait for him!

ISAIAH 30:18

I go through life as a transient on his way to eternity, made in the image of God but with that image debased, needing to be taught how to meditate, to worship, to think.

DONALD COGGAN

in His Word. Here we find rest in the safe pasture of our Shepherd's sanctifying provision, trusting the Lord to complete the work He has begun in us as we keep our focus on Him. Realizing this profound truth—*God has fully forgiven and accepted us! The Lord loves us and wants to spend time with us! Glory to the Master now and forever! Yes!*—radically rearranges our life plans and priorities.

During my prayer time one morning, I began thinking about how a miniscule marigold seed can change into a three-foot-tall flower. I pictured the ivory-and-black-striped sliver springing to life after it had been carefully planted in the ground, awakening from its dormant state only after it had been covered with soil and had received sufficient moisture. In my mind's eye I could see the slender green shoot pressing its way out into the surrounding earth; the life of the flower had begun.

This process, called germination, heralds the beginning of a brand-new creation. Eventually the seed itself dies as the life within manifests itself in a stalk, roots, leaves, and finally a flower. The gardener's desired outcome, measured by an abundant display of brilliant blossoms above ground, must be preceded by earlier hidden phases of development beneath the ground's surface.

As I contemplated this natural process, I better understood something that had always puzzled and amazed me. It really is possible to become a brand-new person inside at the moment Christ enters one's life, although being conformed to His image is an ongoing process, not completed until after one's body dies. It's as though a kind of spiritual germination occurred when, through faith, I believed God's Word and welcomed Jesus into my heart. On an unseen level, I actually was buried with Him and was brought back to life as a new creation right then and there by His life-giving power. Checking in my dictionary, I wasn't surprised to discover that one of the meanings of the word *germinate* is "to create; to cause to come into existence."

I pondered about this for some time, seeing once more why the days I am walking through are barely the beginning of my life in God. I'm still being transformed daily into the person the Lord has lovingly created me to be. That's when it hit me, all at once, as I considered the dramatic difference between the seed and the flower: *The person I will one day be is even more different from who I am now than a full-grown flower is from its original seed.* This life I'm living here is playing out in a shadow land as I heed God's call to keep pressing toward higher ground.

This realization began to reshape my thinking and outlook from the inside out. Even so, living in a culture that exalts worldly goods, high-profile achievements, and ideal body contours sometimes causes me to forget the fleeting nature of my earthly surroundings. When I neglect to keep eternity in view, I grow impatient, frustrated, and self-critical. I find myself thinking and behaving as if this germinal phase is *it*. Without due care and attention, I rearrange my priorities and spontaneously start sprouting off in an opposing direction.

But when I consider who I am and where I'm going, God speaks to me through His Word and challenges me to ask myself what really matters in light of eternity. Where I live today? How much money I earn this year? What color of lipstick I wear tomorrow? (At times I actually laugh at myself, chuckling at the thought of a garden full of seeds taking pride in their dissolving, decaying husks or their dark underground dwelling places. I suppose it's not too different from how we must appear to the angels appointed to watch over each earthbound creature who has yet to enter heaven's glory!)

If I believe my life here on earth is *just the beginning* of my life in Christ, why would I choose to live by any standard that divides my mind and heart over things that won't last? Instead, why wouldn't I love the Lord with my whole being as I wait for Him? If I want my identity to become deeply rooted in Christ as I grow toward heaven,

In God there is no hunger that needs to be filled, only plenteousness that desires to give.

C. S. Lewis

Since, O my soul, thou art capable of God, woe to thee if thou contentest thyself with anything but God.

Francis de Sales

O taste the Lord, and see how sweet He is. The man that trusts in Him lives still in bliss.

Sir John Davies

why would I neglect God's bountiful provision and settle for counterfeit daily bread?

When I slow down long enough to truly *wait* upon the Lord in His Word, taking time out to "be still and know" my God and Savior (Ps. 46:10), setting my mind "on things above, not on earthly things" (Col. 3:2), I realize all over again that I am an offshoot of my risen King, stretching with my whole being toward Jesus.

The Word of God takes on new meaning, reviving my heart, soul, mind, and body as I feast upon its life-giving truth.

Loving others liberates my life from its self-enclosed spaces.

Serving Christ puts into action my convictions about what it means to be my Creator's handiwork, designed with God's divine purpose in mind.

Yes, though I am still far from perfect, I am nevertheless a new creation as I yield, trust, abide—wait—longing to burst forth into full bloom under the Gardener's gentle hand. Living now within my true element, I desire to grow in God's grace with greater understanding, inching toward that day when I will arise in resurrection from an earthly grave and at last see my beautiful Savior face to face. "So then, just as you received Christ Jesus as Lord, continue to live in him, rooted and built up in him, strengthened in the faith as you were taught, and overflowing with thankfulness" (Col. 2:7).

FOCUS POINT➢ The patient waiting we practice in the Lord's presence revives our commitment to Christ and fills our hearts with holy passion.

Can you believe today that God loves you with an everlasting love and that He is calling you to receive and use the gifts He has given you for His glory? Can you walk away, step by step, from the shame of the past, regardless of its cause, and build your confidence on Christ—the wondrous gift of God's love and grace?

No matter what stage of development we are in, we grow in God when we lift our eyes toward our King and wait upon Him in His Word with receptive hearts. Hannah Whitall Smith gave this sage advice:

> See to it that you are planted in grace, and then let the Divine Husbandman cultivate you in His own way and by His own means. Put yourselves out into the sunshine of His presence, and let the dew of heaven come down upon you, and see what will be the result.
>
> Open wide every avenue of your being to receive the blessed influences your Divine Husbandman may bear upon you. Bask in the sunshine of His love. Drink of the waters of His goodness. Keep your face upturned to Him as the flowers do to the sun. *Look*, and your soul shall live and grow.[4]

As our steady growth continues under our Master's watchful, loving care, we are strengthened and sustained by His absolute provision, just as He promised. Just as our sovereign Redeemer progressively redirects our appetites, he also reshapes our entire attitude—not only our overall feelings, opinions, and outlook, but the whole unseen orientation of our hearts, minds, and souls. He changes the hidden inclination of our thoughts, the private posture of our souls, and the habitual disposition of our hearts.

"One thing have I desired of the LORD, that will I seek after; that I may dwell in the house of the LORD all the days of my life, to behold the beauty of the LORD, and to inquire in his temple," exclaimed David (Ps. 27:4 KJV). In David's focused inclination, we see more clearly what a receptive attitude toward God looks like.

When we patiently wait upon Jesus, sitting at His feet and gazing upon His beauty in the secret domain of our hearts, we receive our blessed Savior

I have loved you with an everlasting love; I have drawn you with loving-kindness.

JEREMIAH 31:3

Our joy as Christians is not based on circumstances but rather in being in God's will and doing what we were created to do.

JILL BRISCOE

Know that even when you are in the kitchen, God moves among the pots and pans.

TERESA OF AVILA

and Lord in the innermost place of our desire—recognizing His claim upon us, laying our lives before His altar, caressing His feet, seeking His face, feeding upon His Word, weeping with joy, adoring His majesty, partaking of His mystery, seeking the one thing that matters. As we inwardly sit before the Lord, listening to His Word, we begin to see why "only one thing is necessary"; as we learn to choose what is best for our souls, we rejoice that "it shall not be taken away" from us (Luke 10:42 NEB).

The language of devotion we share with Jesus springs from our love for Him. Self-monitoring ceases. Doing things the "right" way no longer matters. Singing perfectly on key, saying a well-worded prayer, and any other such attempts at self-centered performance become meaningless. As we gaze upon the Lord with eyes of faith from the shadowy plane of the here and now, we lift our hearts in His presence toward His glorious eternal throne.

Setting out to discover the joy of one-on-one fellowship with Christ can be somewhat intimidating at first. Where do we start? What do we say? What do we sing? How long do we pray? How do we obediently "listen to the Word" in order to hear Christ speaking to us? Where do we look to find Jesus when He is utterly invisible to our all-too-human eyes?

The search is less complicated than it may seem: We simply start by *looking*. Then we keep on looking. Our communion with Christ does not depend on a technique or a formula—it depends on a relationship. "When God finds a [person] that rests in Him and is not easily moved," noted Catherine of Genoa, "He gives the joy of His presence, which entirely absorbs the soul."

By single-mindedly diving into the depths of the Word and waiting upon God within it, we learn that God's call to the life above is not just for noteworthy spiritual figures like Catherine of Genoa. It's for everyday saints like you and me.

"Look to the LORD and his strength; seek his face always," emphasized the psalmist, echoing the words of an earlier Old Testament writer (Ps. 105:4; 1 Chron. 16:11). "But if from there you seek the LORD your God, you will find him if you look for him with all your heart and with all your soul," Moses challenged the Israelites as they faced Canaan's border (Deut. 4:29).

These same Bible verses encourage us to look for the Lord today by turning our eyes and ears of faith toward Christ with tenacious determination. Through this hidden inclination of our hearts and souls, we seek God and His kingdom with the eyes of faith. We resolutely take our thoughts off our circumstances and set them on things above.

> FOCUS POINT➢ Because the Word of God is alive within us, we can experience joy and satisfaction as we wait with real hope for the life to come.

Through the expectant waiting we inwardly practice day by day as we feed upon God's Word, we lift the eyes and ears of our hearts toward our Lord in the company of heaven. In the Bible we learn that there is great benefit in this kind of inward *waiting*.

In the following list of Scriptures, the words highlighted in bold print are based on the same Hebrew word *qawâ*. In English *qawâ* is translated according to several different meanings (to hope for, wait for, look for; expect; put trust in; to wait patiently, wait eagerly), underscoring the vital connection between these related aspects of our soul's expectant posture. The attitude of our whole being is involved as we turn our thoughts and desires toward God.[5] In these verses, *qawâ* may appear as *look*, *wait*, *trust*, or *hope*, depending on the Bible translation.

> *He gives vigour to the weary, new strength to the exhausted. Young men may grow weary and faint, even in their prime they may stumble and fall; but those who* **look** *to the* LORD *will win*

I have put my soul, as a blank, into the hands of Jesus Christ my Redeemer, and desired Him to write upon it what He pleases. I know it will be His own image.

GEORGE WHITEFIELD

Hold everything earthly with a loose hand.

C. H. SPURGEON

All that the believer can attain of spiritual consolation in this life is but a taste.

DAVID DICKSON

new strength, they will grow wings like eagles; they will run and not be weary; they will march on and never grow faint (Isa. 40:29-31 NEB).

Wait *for the LORD; be of good courage, and he shall strengthen thine heart.* ***Wait****, I say, on the LORD (Ps. 27:14 KJV).*

I will praise you forever for what you have done; in your name I will **hope**, *for your name is good. I will praise you in the presence of your saints (Ps. 52:9).*

I ***waited*** *patiently for the LORD to help me, and he turned to me and heard my cry. He lifted me out of the pit of despair, out of the mud and mire. He set my feet on solid ground and steadied me as I walked along. He has given me a new song to sing, a hymn of praise to our God. Many will see what he has done and be astounded. They will put their trust in the LORD (Ps. 40:1-4 NLT).*

Wait *for the LORD, and he will deliver you (Prov. 20:22).*

Surely this is our God; we **trusted** *in him and he saved us. This is the LORD, we* **trusted** *in him; let us rejoice and be glad in his salvation (Isa. 25:9).*

Do any of the worthless idols of the nations bring rain? Do the skies themselves send down showers? No, it is you, O LORD our God. Therefore our **hope** *is in you, for you are the one who does all this (Jer. 14:22).*

Wait *for the LORD and keep his way (Ps. 37:34).*

Guard my life and rescue me; let me not be put to shame, for I take refuge in you. May integrity and uprightness protect me, because my **hope** *is in you (Ps. 25:20-21).*

Because of the LORD's great love we are not consumed, for his compassions never fail. They are new every morning; great is your faithfulness. I say to myself, "The LORD is my portion; therefore I will **wait** *for him." The LORD is good to those whose* **hope** *is in him, to the one who seeks him; it is good to* **wait** *quietly for the salvation of the LORD (Lam. 3:22-26).*

> *I will **wait** for the LORD, who is hiding his face from the house of Jacob. I will put my **trust** in him (Isa. 8:17).*
>
> *I **wait** for the LORD, my soul **waits**, and in his word I put my **hope**. My soul **waits** for the LORD more than watchmen wait for the morning, more than watchmen wait for the morning (Ps. 130:5).*
>
> *I **trust** in you for salvation, O LORD! (Gen. 49:18 NLT).*
>
> *Therefore, return to your God, observe kindness and justice, and **wait** for your God continually (Hos. 12:6 NASB).*
>
> *To You, O LORD, I lift up my soul. O my God, in You I trust. Do not let me be ashamed; do not let my enemies exult over me. Indeed, none of those who **wait** for You will be ashamed; those who deal treacherously without cause will be ashamed. Make me know Your ways, O LORD; teach me Your paths. Lead me in Your truth and teach me, for You are the God of my salvation; for You I **wait** all the day (Ps. 25:1-5 NASB).*

Actively waiting upon the Lord with expectant hope makes us more sensitive to the "gentle whisper" of God's voice. In this way the Word of God supplies life-giving nourishment as we feed on Christ.

"Be still before the LORD and wait patiently for him," David advised those seeking God's strength and wisdom (Ps. 37:7). This silent wait-

Let those who thoughtfully consider the brevity of life remember the length of eternity.

THOMAS KEN

We need no wings to go in search of Him, but have only to find a place where we can be alone and look upon Him present with us.

TERESA OF AVILA

If we hope for something we do not see, then we exercise patience in waiting.

GUERRIC OF IGNY

ing inclines our soul's appetite toward what is worth wanting. Dietrich Bonhoeffer commented on the work of silence:

> Silence is the simple stillness of the individual under the Word of God. We are silent before hearing the Word because our thoughts are already directed to the Word, as a child is quiet when he enters his father's room. We are silent after hearing the Word because the Word is still speaking and dwelling within us. We are silent at the beginning of the day because God should have the first word, and we are silent before going to sleep because the last word also belongs to God. We keep silence solely for the sake of the Word, and therefore not in order to show disregard for the Word but rather to honor and receive it.
>
> Silence is nothing else but waiting for God's Word and coming from God's Word with a blessing. But everybody knows this is something that needs to be practiced and learned, in these days when talkativeness prevails. Real silence, real stillness, really holding one's tongue comes only as the sober consequence of spiritual stillness.[6]

FOCUS POINT➢ The solitary waiting we practice in the Lord's presence inclines our innermost appetite and attitude to what is worth wanting, having, and desiring.

In turning our eyes and ears toward Jesus—waiting in silence while taking in God's Word—we taste and see God's goodness. When we direct our heart's desires toward Christ and depend on Him rather than on someone or something else to satisfy our soul's deep longing for relationship, our love for others will involve more giving and less taking.

Without a doubt, meditating on God's Word, sitting down to the spiritual feast, brings spiritual growth. But how can we possibly taste, chew, swallow, and digest the meal He has provided if we continually keep ourselves on the go, consistently deny our soul's need for rest and stillness, and rarely stop to listen to our Shepherd's voice? No wonder we experience such unsettling hunger pangs, distracting our hearts, minds, and souls from the one thing that really matters! Yet it doesn't have to be this way.

Cultivating our private practice of the classic spiritual disciplines such as prayer, praise, worship, solitude, study, fasting, and meditation on the Word of God prevents "the earthly things" from filling our inner emptiness and specifically aims our soul's hunger toward heaven. We mindfully turn our heart's desires toward our Beloved as we wait for Him and lovingly embrace our Savior with genuine intimacy when we find Him.

"The prophet Elijah did not encounter God in the mighty wind or in the earthquake or in the fire, but in the still small voice (see 1 Kings 19:9-13)," explained writer and theology professor Henri J. M. Nouwen. "Through the practice of a spiritual discipline we become attentive to that small voice and willing to respond when we hear it."[7] Nouwen's description of our vital need for this discipline offers us motivation:

> It is clear that we are usually surrounded by so much noise that it is hard to truly hear God when he is speaking to us. We have often become deaf, unable to know when God calls us and unable to understand in which direction he calls us. Thus our lives have become absurd.
>
> In the word *absurd* we find the Latin word *surdus*, which means "deaf." A spiritual life requires discipline because we need to learn to listen to God, who constantly speaks but whom we seldom hear.
>
> When, however, we learn to listen, our lives become obedient lives. The word *obedient* comes from the Latin word *audire*, which means "listening." A spiritual disci-

Waiting exercises our grace; waiting tries our faith; therefore, wait on in hope; for though the promise tarry, it can never come too late.

C. H. Spurgeon

In this world, things that are naturally to endure for a long time are the slowest in reaching maturity.

Vincent de Paul

He who gets wisdom loves his own soul; he who cherishes understanding prospers.

Proverbs 19:8

> pline is necessary in order to move slowly from an absurd to an obedient life, from a life filled with noisy worries to a life in which there is some free inner space where we can listen to our God and follow his guidance.
>
> Jesus' life was a life of obedience. He was always listening to the Father, always attentive to his voice, always alert for his directions. Jesus was "all ear." That is true prayer: being all ear for God. The core of all prayer is indeed listening, obediently standing in the presence of God.
>
> A spiritual discipline, therefore, is the concentrated effort to create some inner and outer space in our lives where this obedience can be practiced. Through a spiritual discipline we prevent the world from filling our lives to such an extent that there is no place left to listen. A spiritual discipline sets us free to pray or, to say it better, allows the Spirit of God to pray in us.[8]

The practice of a spiritual discipline does not automatically appear after our conversion. It requires the unreserved sacrifice of an open, willing heart. "God nowhere tells us to give up things for the sake of giving them up. He tells us to give them up for the sake of the only thing worth having—life with Himself," affirmed Oswald Chambers.[9] *A thing is worth what someone is willing to pay for it.*

A spiritual discipline is a learned skill that requires focused effort on our part—the practice of obediently turning our eyes and ears to God in His Word; the hospitality of our hearts through which we expectantly welcome the Lord and greet His presence in prayer with genuine thanksgiving; the concentrated, private exercise of our faith at the center of our public lives where we commune with God.

The solitary practice of spiritual disciplines occurs on the unseen side of discipleship whenever we follow Jesus' clear command to *go away* by ourselves, *shut the door* behind us, and *pray* to our Father secretly (Matt. 6:6 NLT). Our silent pursuit of God need not drive us to a monastery to produce lasting benefit. We can reap the fruit of fellowship with the Lord *wherever* and *whenever* we make the choice to set our minds upon His Word. *"You will seek me and find me when you seek me with all your heart,"* He promised (Jer. 29:13). He is waiting to meet us even now.

Our soul waits for the LORD; He is our help and our shield. For our heart rejoices in Him, because we trust in His holy name. (Ps. 33:20-21 NASB)

Here I sink before Thee lowly,
Filled with gladness deep and holy,
As with trembling awe and wonder
On Thy mighty work I ponder,
On this banquet's mystery,
On the depths we cannot see;
Far beyond all mortal sight
Lie the secrets of Thy might.

Sun, who all my life dost brighten,
Light, who dost my soul enlighten,
Joy, the sweetest man e'er knoweth,
Fount, whence all my being floweth,
Humbly draw I near to Thee;
Grant that I may worthily
Take this blessed heavenly food,
To Thy praise, and to my good.

Jesus, Bread of Life from heaven,
Never be thou vainly given,
Nor I to my hurt invited
Be Thy love with love requited;
Let me learn its depths indeed,
While on Thee my soul doth feed;
Let me, here so richly blest,
Be hereafter too Thy guest.[10]

—LYRA ANGLICANA, "EATING AND DRINKING WITH CHRIST" (1864)

We need never shout across the spaces to an absent God. He is nearer than our own soul, closer than our most secret thoughts.

A. W. TOZER

Second only to suffering, waiting may be the greatest teacher and trainer in godliness, maturity, and genuine spirituality most of us ever encounter.

RICHARD HENDRIX

It is better to live rich than die rich.

SAMUEL JOHNSON

Focus points

➢ The patient waiting we practice in the Lord's presence revives our commitment to Christ and fills our hearts with holy passion.

➢ Because the Word of God is alive within us, we can experience joy and satisfaction as we wait with real hope for the life to come.

➢ The solitary waiting we practice in the Lord's presence inclines our innermost appetite and attitude to what is worth wanting, having, and desiring.

Nourishment from God's Word

As Jesus and his disciples were on their way, he came to a village where a woman named Martha opened her home to him. She had a sister called Mary, who sat at the Lord's feet listening to what he said. But Martha was distracted by all the preparations that had to be made. She came to him and asked, "Lord, don't you care that my sister has left me to do the work by myself? Tell her to help me!"

"Martha, Martha," the Lord answered, "you are worried and upset about many things, but only one thing is needed. Mary has chosen what is better, and it will not be taken from her."

—LUKE 10:38-42

Six days before the Passover, Jesus arrived at Bethany, where Lazarus lived, whom Jesus had raised from the dead. Here a dinner was given in Jesus' honor. Martha served, while Lazarus was among those reclining at the table with him. Then Mary took about a pint of pure nard, an expensive perfume; she poured it on Jesus' feet and wiped his feet with her hair. And the house was filled with the fragrance of the perfume.

—JOHN 12:1-3

If you love me, obey my commandments. And I will ask the Father, and he will give you another Counselor, who will never leave you. He is the Holy Spirit, who leads into all truth. The world at large cannot receive him, because it isn't looking for him and doesn't recognize him. But you do, because he lives with you now and later will be in you. No, I will not abandon you as orphans—I will come to you. In just a little while the world will not see me again, but you will. For I will live again, and you will, too. When I am raised to life again, you will know that I am in my Father, and you are in me, and I am in you. Those who obey my commandments are the ones who love me. And because they love me, my Father will love them, and I will love them. And I will reveal myself to each one of them.

—JOHN 14:15-21 NLT

LORD, you have assigned me my portion and my cup;
you have made my lot secure.
The boundary lines have fallen for me in pleasant places;
surely I have a delightful inheritance.
I will praise the LORD who counsels me;
even at night my heart instructs me.
I have set the LORD always before me.
Because he is at my right hand, I will not be shaken.
Therefore my heart is glad and my tongue rejoices;
my body also will rest secure,
because you will not abandon me to the grave,
nor will you let your Holy One see decay.
You have made known to me the path of life;
you will fill me with joy in your presence,
with eternal pleasures at your right hand.

—PSALM 16:5-11

Like an apple tree among the trees of the forest
is my lover among the young men.
I delight to sit in his shade, and his fruit is sweet to my taste.
He has taken me to the banquet hall, and his banner over me is love.
Strengthen me with raisins, refresh me with apples,
for I am faint with love.
His left arm is under my head, and his right arm embraces me.

Listen! My lover!
Look! Here he comes, leaping across the mountains,
bounding over the hills.
My lover is like a gazelle or a young stag.
Look! There he stands behind our wall,

gazing through the windows, peering though the lattice.
My lover spoke and said to me, "Arise, my darling,
my beautiful one, and come with me.
See! The winter is past; the rains are over and gone.
Flowers appear on the earth; the season of singing has come,
the cooing of doves is heard in our land.
The fig tree forms its early fruit;
the blossoming vines spread their fragrance.
Arise, come my darling; my beautiful one, come with me."

—SONG OF SONGS 2:3-6, 8-13

Reflection Points

1. As I look to the Lord with thanksgiving, I sometimes see . . . .
2. When I feel distant from the Lord, I find it difficult to . . . .
3. My innermost needs for love and fulfillment are best met by . . . .
4. Even though I believe I am growing in grace, I sometimes struggle to feel fully forgiven and accepted by God, especially when . . . .
5. For me, waiting on God's Word in silence means . . . .
6. Entering into communion with Christ from the depths of my heart helps me . . . .
7. If I were to write a psalm at this point in my life, it would say . . . .

Additional Study

—*MEDITATE ON* Psalms 23; 27; 42; 123; 131.

—*READ ABOUT* three biblical women who knew how to wait:

Ruth, the quiet desert traveler, devoted daughter-in-law, and foremother of David's famous family, in Ruth 1:1-18; 3:1-8; 4:13-23. (Interestingly, the name Ruth means "satiation" and "refreshment.")

Esther, Jewish exile-in-disguise, unlikely harem expert, courageous queen of Persia, in Esther 2:2-23; 4:1—5:8; 7:1—8:17.

Anna, a most patient prophetess and devout temple dweller, in Luke 2:25-38. (Is it merely a coincidence the name Anna comes from the Hebrew word for grace? I don't think so!)

—*STUDY* Psalms 34:1-8; 36:5-9; 86:1-13; 107:1-9; Matthew 6:1-18; 7:7-13; Ephesians 1:3-23; 3:16-21; 1 Thessalonians 5:16-24.

—*MEMORIZE* Psalms 33:20-21; 34:4-5; 121:1-2; 130:5; 138:8; Isaiah 30:15; Jeremiah 35:21; 2 Corinthians 4:16; Ephesians 5:1; Revelation 22:17.

Suggested Exercises

• After reading and reflecting on the psalm passage below, copy the bold-faced words in your journal, leaving ample space for taking notes and writing down your thoughts between entries.

Using the brief chart that follows as a guideline, describe in your own words the meaning, purpose, value, and result associated with each waiting-related activity David practiced. Think about and make a list of the possible impact of these spiritual activities on one's heart, mind, body, and soul, as eloquently expressed in these verses and elsewhere in the Bible. You may find it helpful to consult a concordance, dictionary, and/or other Bible study tool as you do this exercise.

Summarize your thoughts by writing about how these activities have promoted your growth in God and enhanced your understanding of His love and grace. When you have finished, find a durable sheet of paper, write down this passage from Psalm 27, and display it prominently as a personal reminder in a place where you will see it often—your bedside table by the alarm clock, your bathroom mirror, the refrigerator door, or your computer desk perhaps?

O God, thou art my God, I ***seek*** *thee early*
with a heart that thirsts for thee
and a body wasted with longing for thee,
like a dry and thirsty land where there is no water.
So ***longing****, I* ***come before*** *thee in the sanctuary*
to ***look upon*** *thy power and glory.*
Thy true love is better than life;
therefore I will ***sing*** *your praises.*
And so I ***bless*** *thee all my life*
and in thy name ***lift up my hands in prayer****.*
I am satisfied as with a rich and sumptuous feast

and ***wake the echoes with thy praise****.*
When I ***call thee to mind*** *upon my bed*
and ***think*** *on thee in the watches of the night,*
remembering *how thou hast been my help*
and that I am safe in the shadow of thy wings,
then I humbly ***follow*** *thee with all my heart,*
and thy right hand is my support.

—PSALM 63:1-8 NEB

Meaning: What do you think was expressed to God through this activity? What did this action seem to signify or indicate?

Purpose: What might the reasons for doing this activity have been? What does the goal of this activity appear to be to you?

Value: What do you believe the worth, importance, or usefulness of this activity may have been?

Result: What was the outcome of this activity? What did David come to realize, know, experience, or understand as a consequence of pursuing, praising, or perceiving God in this manner?

• In the New Testament we see women's actions and attitudes toward Christ expressed through a variety of word pictures. As you look up the ten examples listed here, observe the women's actions and attitudes shown in each passage, whether stated or implied. Notice where Jesus is—what is He doing and saying, if anything? After you have completed this review, record your thoughts and observations. (Please note: The actions and attitudes I've listed here are based on my own observations of the passages as found in the following Bible translations: King James Version, New International Version, New Living Translation, New English Bible, New American Standard Bible, Phillips, and *The Message*. If you find something different, don't hesitate to amend this chart as desired.)

1.

Verses:	Luke 1:39-45
Name:	Elizabeth
Central Event:	Mary's visit with Elizabeth
Location of Event:	Elizabeth's home
Action:	Greeting, blessing, exclaiming, crying out, being filled with the Holy Spirit
Attitude:	Glad, joyful, exuberant, thankful, respectful, happy; her preborn baby John leaps for joy
Description of Jesus:	In Mary's womb

Your thoughts and observations:

2.

Verses:	Luke 1:46-55
Name:	Mary, Jesus' mother
Central Event:	Mary's soul magnifying the Lord
Location of Event:	Elizabeth's home
Action:	Magnifying, exalting, blessing, glorifying, singing, praising, rejoicing
Attitude:	Worshipful, amazed, humble, happy, gracious, joyful, grateful, awed, satisfied
Description of Jesus:	In her womb

Your thoughts and observations:

3.

Verses: Luke 2:21-38

Name: Anna

Central Event: Jesus' circumcision

Location of Event: The temple

Action: Walking toward Jesus, observing, waiting, worshiping, fasting, serving, praying, prophesying, giving thanks, discerning, telling people about Jesus, talking about the redemption of Jerusalem

Attitude: Steadfast; understanding; obedient; thankful; full of praise, wisdom, and devotion; set apart for God

Description of Jesus: In Simeon's arms

Your thoughts and observations:

4.

Verses: John 4:7-42

Name: The Samaritan woman

Central Event: Jesus visits Samaria

Location of Event: Jacob's well

Action: Questioning, listening, thinking, replying, seeking, explaining, reacting, recalling, talking, perceiving, confessing, seeing, hearing, knowing, believing, evangelizing (telling others about Jesus, people believing in Christ after hearing her testimony); walking toward Jesus, standing or sitting with the Messiah at the well, returning to town to tell others what she had seen and heard

Attitude: Surprised, inquisitive, alert, candid, informed, honest, hopeful, amazed

Description of Jesus: Traveling to Galilee, sitting and resting on the well, staying with the Samaritans for two days, making a

	request, answering questions, voicing commands, sharing truth, declaring His identity, doing the will of His Father and finishing His Father's work, proclaiming and gathering the harvest

Your thoughts and observations:

5.

Verses:	Luke 8:1-3
Name:	Mary of Magdala, Joanna, Suzanna, and others
Central Event:	Jesus proclaims and preaches the kingdom of God
Location of Event:	On the road, in cities and villages
Action:	Following Jesus, walking, ministering, supporting, helping, contributing, healing of diseases, releasing from demonic bondage, being led by the Lord
Attitude:	Generous, disciplined, committed
Description of Jesus:	Traveling throughout villages and cities, leading His disciples and followers, proclaiming and preaching the good news of the kingdom of God

Your thoughts and observations:

6.

Verses:	Luke 10:38-42
Name:	Mary of Bethany
Central Event:	Jesus visits Martha and Mary
Location of Event:	Her home
Action:	Listening to Jesus, learning, waiting, looking, focusing, feasting, growing spiritually
Attitude:	Drawing near Christ, receptive, calm, content, aware,

	attentive, constant, obedient, well-positioned, firmly planted, all ears
Description of Jesus:	On his way to Jerusalem, welcomed by Martha, heard by Mary, feeding, teaching, explaining, counseling, commending

Your thoughts and observations:

7.

Verses:	John 12:1-8
Name:	Mary of Bethany
Central Event:	Dinner with Lazarus six days before Passover (Palm Sunday Eve)
Location of Event:	Her home
Action:	Kneeling at Jesus' feet, anointing and massaging His feet with perfume and wiping them with her hair, believing, anticipating
Attitude:	Worshiping, loving, adoring, honoring, sacrificing, glorifying, responsive to the Holy Spirit, humble, gracious, inspired, invested, fervent, devoted, single-minded, submitted, surrendered, abandoned
Description of Jesus:	Arrives at Bethany; visits Lazarus, Martha, and Mary; reclines at table with Lazarus; accepts, affirms, and defends Mary's sacrifice; rebukes Judas Iscariot; refers to His death; for the second time shields Mary from criticism and commends her action and attitude

Your thoughts and observations:

8.

Verses:	John 19:16-42
Name:	Mary, Jesus' mother; Mary, Clopas' wife; Mary of Magdala
Central Event:	Jesus' crucifixion
Location of Event:	By the cross
Action:	Standing near the cross, looking, beholding, staying, enduring, witnessing, watching
Attitude:	Grief-stricken, bewildered, shocked
Description of Jesus:	Bearing the cross to Golgotha; being ridiculed, crucified, bartered over, and buried; caring for His mother; suffering, dying, redeeming

Your thoughts and observations:

9.

Verses:	John 20:1-18
Name:	Mary of Magdala
Central Event:	Jesus' resurrection
Location of Event:	At Jesus' empty tomb
Action:	Visiting the tomb, stooping down to look for Jesus, facing Jesus, running back to the disciples, looking, leaving, hurrying, panting, returning, persevering, crying, searching, waiting, listening, speaking, presuming, encountering, hearing, recognizing, exclaiming, calling out, clinging, adoring, witnessing, obeying, carrying the good news
Attitude:	Devoted, heartbroken, faithful, single-minded, grief-stricken, tenacious, perplexed, awestruck, joyous, changed forever
Description of Jesus:	Standing by the tomb, asking a question, saying Mary's name, explaining why she could not cling to

	Him, describing His coming ascension, commissioning Mary to "go" and "tell," welcoming Mary into His Father's family, revealing her reconciliation with God

Your thoughts and observations:

10.

Verses:	Acts 1:4 -14
Name:	Mary, Jesus' mother; "the women"
Central Event:	Jesus' ascension
Location of Event:	Mount of Olives; the Upper Room
Action:	Waiting upon Christ at His ascension and after, returning to Jerusalem, lodging in the Upper Room, listening, learning, watching, witnessing, looking, waiting, obeying, meeting together, continuing in one accord, praying constantly
Attitude:	Expectant, focused, full of faith and hope
Description of Jesus:	Gathers everyone, commands them not to leave Jerusalem as they wait for the Holy Spirit's baptism, teaches about the kingdom of God and commissions disciples, ascends into heaven

Your thoughts and observations:

Closing Prayers

O eternal God, make my body and soul to be a holy temple, purified for the habitation of Thy Holy Spirit. Cast out of it, O Lord, all worldly affections, all covetous desires; let it be a place of prayer and holy meditation, of pure intentions, and zealous desires of pleas-

ing Thee; so that, loving Thee above all the world, and worshipping Thee continually in humblest adoration, I may be prepared to glorify Thee to all eternity in heaven; through Jesus Christ our Lord—Amen.[11]

—JEREMY TAYLOR
(1613-1667)

Speak, Lord, for Thy servant heareth. Grant us ears to hear, eyes to see, wills to obey, hearts to love; then declare what Thou wilt, command what Thou wilt, demand what Thou wilt—Amen.[12]

—CHRISTINA ROSSETTI
(1830-1894)

> *But let all those who seek thee be jubilant and rejoice in thee; and let those who long for thy saving help ever cry, "All glory to the LORD!" (Psalm 40:16 NEB)*

FOOD FOR THOUGHT

"One thing." Divided aims tend to distraction, weakness, disappointment. The man of one book is eminent; the man of one pursuit is successful. Let all our affections be bound up in one affection, and that affection set upon heavenly things.

"Have I desired." What we cannot at once attain, it is well to desire. God judges us very much by the desire of our hearts. He who rides a lame horse is not blamed by his master for want of speed, if he makes all the haste he can, and would make more if he could; God takes the will for the deed with his children.

"Of the Lord." This is the right target for desires; this is the well into which to dip our buckets; this is the door to knock at, the bank to draw upon. Desire of men, and lie on the dunghill with Lazarus; desire of the Lord, and be carried of angels into Abraham's bosom. Our desires of the Lord should be sanctified, humble, constant, submissive, fervent, and it is well if, as with the psalmist, they are all molten into one cause. Under David's painful circumstances we might have expected him to desire repose, safety, and a thousand other good things, but, no, he has set his heart on the pearl and leaves the rest.

"That will I seek after." Holy desires must lead to resolute action. The old proverb says, "wishers and woulders are never good housekeepers," and "wishing never fills a sack." Desires are seeds which must be sown in the good soil of activity, or they

will yield no harvest. We shall find our desires to be like clouds without rain, unless followed up by practical endeavors.

"That I may dwell in the house of the Lord all the days of my life." For the sake of communion with the King, David longed to dwell always in the palace; so far from being wearied with the services of the Tabernacle, he longed to be constantly engaged in them, as his life-long pleasure. He desired above all things to be one of the household of God, a home-born child, living at home with his Father. This is our deepest wish, only we extend it to those days of our immortal life which have not yet dawned. We pine for our Father's house above, the home of our souls; if we may but dwell there forever, we care but little for the goods or ills of this poor life. "Jerusalem the golden" is the one and only goal of our heart's longings.

"To behold the beauty of the Lord." An exercise both for earthly and heavenly worshippers. We must not enter the assemblies of the saints in order to see and be seen, or merely to hear the minister; we must repair to the gatherings of the righteous, intent upon the gracious object of learning more of the loving Father, more of the glorified Jesus, more of the mysterious Spirit, in order that we may more lovingly admire, and the more reverently adore our glorious God. What a word is that, "the beauty of the Lord!" Think of it, dear reader! Better far—behold it by faith! What a sight will that be when every faithful follower of Jesus shall behold "the King in his beauty!" Oh, for the infinitely blessed vision!

"And to enquire in his temple." We should make our visits to the Lord's house enquirers' meetings. Not seeking sinners alone, but assured saints should be enquirers. We must enquire as to the will of God and how we may do it—as to our interest in the heavenly city, and how we may be more assured of it. We shall not need to make enquiries in heaven, for there we shall know even as we are known; but meanwhile we should sit at Jesus' feet and awaken all our faculties to learn of him.[13]

—C. H. SPURGEON
(1834-1892)

CHAPTER SIX

FACE TO FACE: *When Will We Gain Full Satisfaction?*

Very near is the LORD to those who call to him, who call to him in singleness of heart.

—PSALM 145:18 NEB

Everything we call a trial, a sorrow, a duty: believe me. That angel's hand is there, the gift is there, and the wonder of an overshadowing Presence. Our joys too: be not content with them as joys. They too conceal diviner gifts. Life is so full of meaning and purpose, so full of beauty beneath its covering, that you will find earth but cloaks your heaven. Courage, then, to claim it, that is all! But courage you have, and the knowledge that we are pilgrims wending through unknown country on our way home.[1]

—FRA ANGELICO (1387-1455)

Look at the Lord Jesus firmly and fixedly, never letting your gaze wander elsewhere; and whatever temporal objects come between you and your Lord, look right through them, as though through a mist, and fix your eyes and heart upon Him and Him alone. Whatever condition you find yourself in, do not let either earth or heaven hide Him.[2]

—JOHN HARRIS

You still the hunger of those you cherish . . . . and I—in righteousness I will see your face; when I awake, I will be satisfied with seeing your likeness.

—PSALM 17:14-15

In our garage behind a stack of boxes containing Christmas decorations, fabric scraps, and unmatched socks, a cherry wood bed frame leans against a painted brick wall. Dust has coated it, thickly gathered on the edges, but the hearts and flowers carved into the headboard can still be seen winding their way across its top border. The mattress has been tossed out, and two legs are splintered, making the old frame incapable of supporting its side boards. Yet in spite of the bed's condition, we continue to keep it. We will probably never part with it. Our first child was born in this bed, and when I look at its carved borders, I remember her coming into the world.

I think about the day my mother called me on the phone and said, "I want to buy the bed my first grandchild will be born in." Soon afterward she drove half an hour to the farm we were living on and took me to an antique store to browse among its stockpile of meticulously polished treasures.

Up and down the aisles we stalked, peeking behind tall pine cupboards, massive walnut buffets, and ornate oak cabinets. We didn't see many beds in our casual search, and the ones we did look at were either outrageously expensive brass creations or too small for a double-sized mattress. Then on the far wall of the store we saw a bed we both agreed would be the perfect choice. At only fifty dollars, the piece was a good bargain, so my mom immediately proposed that I pick out a dresser to go with it.

When the two pieces arrived, they were a welcome addition to our small home, which was primarily decorated with hand-me-downs from our families, Salvation Army artifacts, and garage-sale discoveries. Once the bed's varnish was removed, the cherry wood's beauty fully revealed itself, absorbing the wax I rubbed into it with ease. With our child due on June 28, 1972, we set up and began sleeping in the birthing bed around the first of that month.

Often I would sit at the edge of the bed and gaze at the borrowed cradle positioned alongside, trying to imagine what our nights would be like having a newborn sleeping in the room near us. I pictured myself feeding and bathing her, taking her for walks, singing to her, telling her stories. My secret daydreams about our expected child were filled with awe and wonder, anxiety and apprehension, softened by hopeful anticipation of realities to come. As springtime gave way to summer, I felt myself blooming inside. The urge to settle in and "nest" was always close at hand.

Because my mother had used the Lamaze method for the birth of my youngest sister in 1963, I was brought up with the belief that having a baby was a natural, normal function of women's sexuality that I need not fear. I can clearly remember sitting on our living room floor, watching my parents practice breathing and relaxation techniques as I questioned how "candle-blowing" eased the whole mysterious process.

A childbirth instructor later cautioned Dave and me to avoid using the word *pain* when referring to the work of birth because the expectation of pain would lead to "failure" of the Lamaze method. We also learned from Dr. Lamaze's book, *Painless Childbirth*, that if performed correctly, his birthing method would entirely eliminate labor pain. A motivational film shown in class offered compelling evidence of this remarkable thesis. So I approached my delivery date with relaxed confidence, expecting it to be the peak experience of my life.

At that time there were no birthing rooms or birthing centers—just surgical rooms containing stainless steel tables fitted with hand straps and leg stirrups. Fathers were just beginning to be allowed to attend their children's births. In many hospitals, mothers and babies were separated after birth for a mandatory twenty-four-hour period; rooming-in was almost nonexistent. Not surprisingly, the U.S. breastfeeding rate still hovered near a record low. These facts guided our decision to have a home

So do not fear, for I am with you; do not be dismayed, for I am your God. I will strengthen you and help you; I will uphold you with my righteous right hand.

Isaiah 41:10

If you do not hope, you will not find out what is beyond your hopes.

Clement of Alexandria

When you see the end of things, you can go through virtually anything to get there.

Peter E. Gillquist

birth after we located a family physician, a former missionary doctor, who offered healthy clients a choice regarding their baby's birth place.

The last weeks of the pregnancy were fairly miserable as my abdomen swelled and my arms ached to hold my baby. Poor sleep, constant pressure, and frequent trips to the bathroom let me know that my womb had reached full capacity. I often wept with frustration, wondering if our baby was ever going to arrive, imagining she would continue to grow ever larger, thinking there would be no end to the heaviness in my abdomen. Then, on the afternoon of our baby's due date, labor finally began.

Following an uncomfortable bout with diarrhea, I noted a tight feeling in my lower abdomen strongly resembling menstrual cramps. The sensation forcefully radiated toward my back in hot waves as it increased in intensity, temporarily stayed tight, and subsequently tapered off. I wondered if it was normal to be feeling this intestinal discomfort in spite of correctly using the breathing and relaxation techniques.

With a certain amount of panic, I phoned the doctor, who briefly evaluated this information, reassured me that everything sounded perfectly normal, and requested that I visit his office as soon as possible for further evaluation.

During the exam, my physician seemed neither concerned nor surprised when I told him I was feeling pain despite using the Lamaze method. After checking the baby's heartbeat and my cervix, which was dilated about six centimeters, he sent Dave and me home, promising he would soon join us. I was excited, apprehensive, and trying very hard not to be nervous.

When we got home, I immediately took off my clothes and stepped into the shower, letting the warm water stream down my aching back. With each contraction, I leaned against the wall and took slow, deep, mammoth breaths, attempting to relieve the growing pressure in my abdomen. It still hurt. At first the pain puzzled me, then annoyed me. Was I doing something wrong? If not, why did it hurt?

Up until this point, my husband's presence as a passive bystander had suited me just fine. Suddenly I wanted him right there, right away, and didn't want him to leave *ever again*. With considerable assistance, I left the shower and curled up in bed, where Dave alternately rubbed my back, helped pace my breathing, joked with the doctor who had come by now, played his guitar, and kept smiling.

How can he actually be singing and laughing at a time like this? I thought as I threw up my orange juice. *Why am I the one that has to go through this? I'm never going have another baby. And maybe not even sex.*

Although the otherness of Dave's masculine design seemed especially distant from my own design during the transition phase of my labor, I knew that having him there next to me was the closest a man could ever come to experiencing the work of birth. Even so, I longed for my husband to reach across the void between us and feel what I was feeling. For a short span of sixty minutes, space and time changed. I often felt helpless to cope with my pain and bewildered by a body I believed should be cooperating with my mind more efficiently during labor. I sincerely wanted to give up, set my uterus on a shelf, shout good riddance, and walk away.

But cope I did. A strange inner strength I hadn't encountered before emerged as I rode the wild, uncontrollable waves of my contractions, willing my body to open up and allow my child safe passage. As I began to push, my whole being was swept along by my womb's surging rhythms, moving my baby down, pressing the muscles of my pelvis open, filling every possible space with an unrelenting natural force. Kneeling, I braced myself against a stack of pillows on our bed. I groaned as my womb intermittently tightened itself from the top down. Between contractions a bliss-

It is not easy to live faithfully in a world full of ambiguities. We have to learn how to make wise choices without needing to be entirely sure.

HENRI NOUWEN

Faith is to believe what you do not yet see; the reward for this faith is to see what you believe.

AUGUSTINE OF HIPPO

In repentance and rest is your salvation, in quietness and trust is your strength.

ISAIAH 30:15

ful two to three minutes of complete rest prepared my mind and body for the hard work ahead.

Outside, through the open windows of our room, I heard the sounds of dogs barking and birds singing. The air was filled with the stillness of summer twilight as the sun began to set. I breathed in its sweet fragrance and let the approaching evening's coolness caress my forehead. How strange it seemed that this was just an ordinary day, packed with ordinary events, while I was completing the most demanding task of my life.

"Not much longer," I heard the doctor saying quietly as he prepared to receive the baby.

Then my husband started to giggle. "I can see the baby's hair!" he announced with glee. "Keep pushing! You can do it, honey! Oh wow . . ."

Dismissing them both with a grimace and a groan, I thought: *I don't care what they say. This isn't a baby—it's some huge, immovable object that has no right to be where it is. I want it out! Now!*

But then a startling thing happened—a most unexpected and amazing thing. As our daughter's head appeared, the pain of giving birth suddenly gave way to an exhilarating sensation of release, then relief. Such blessed relief! When the baby's shoulders came through, the incredible reality of what was taking place hit me full force, all at once, as I felt her arms, her back, her legs slip through in a whoosh, her warm skin so astonishingly smooth.

"It really *is* a baby after all . . . my baby, my baby, my baby," I cooed, gladly reaching out to welcome Joanna as the doctor laid her beside me on the bed.

For the next forty-eight hours, sleep would not come. I felt myself coming fully alive as I became better acquainted with this little one whom I had never met. But I had *known* her. Welcoming Joanna home was simply an extension of maternal hospitality, an expansion of the knowledge I already possessed about the person whose body had sprung to life within my womb many months earlier.

How could it be that this most joyous of occasions had sprung from such intense discomfort? Birth is a bittersweet moment, I found, a time when heaven and earth collide in an extraordinary profusion of possibilities, desires, hopes, dreams, and expectations. So many emotions stirred my heart. A sense of awe that two infinitesimal cells had become our daughter simply overwhelmed me. I smiled and wept, shedding tears of concern while laughing with joy. Simultaneously, I felt a heavy weight of responsibility falling right between my shoulders. I sensed I would never be quite the same woman again.

You may be wondering why I've chosen to describe birth in a book about spiritual satisfaction. There's a good reason. Put simply, it's because my cumulative knowledge about childbearing has deepened my respect and appreciation for another kind of birth process, powerfully described here by the apostle Paul:

> *For we know that all creation has been groaning as in the pains of childbirth right up to the present time. And even we Christians, although we have the Holy Spirit within us as a foretaste of future glory, also groan to be released from pain and suffering. We, too, wait anxiously for that day when God will give us our full rights as his children, including the new bodies he has promised us. Now that we are saved, we eagerly look forward to this freedom. For if you already have something, you don't need to hope for it. But if we look forward to something we don't have yet, we must wait patiently and confidently (Rom. 8:22-25* NLT*).*

Do we really believe these words—that all around us, in any given place, at this very moment creation is groaning loudly like a laboring woman swept up in the tumultuous throes of giving birth?

It is worth a world to have an intimate eternity with Christ.

J. G. BELLETT

In heaven we will praise God "face to face." The current of song will pour straight from us to Him. But we need not wait until then. We can start the singing early.

TIM STAFFORD

I think I see more of Christ than I ever saw; and yet I see but little of what may be seen.

SAMUEL RUTHERFORD

Though it's a bit embarrassing to admit now, I must tell you I was not a calm, collected, quiet birth-giver during the two-and-a-half hour unmedicated pushing phase preceding Joanna's arrival. Just ask Dave.

I grunted. I moaned. I cried out in high-pitched shrieks that seemed like someone else's voice. After my first labor my throat was so sore from making all those alien noises that I lost my voice and ended up whispering off and on for two or three days. Invite any veteran midwife to mimic the sounds of a woman in childbirth, and doubtless she will offer a convincing demonstration of guttural grunts and groans likely to leave you blushing, or thinking about a team of brawny men moving a grand piano up several flights of stairs.

Clearly, an anesthesia-free birth is not a soundless, predictable, easy process. It's a nonstop, labor-intensive, hold-on-to-your-hats kind of experience you can't possibly step out of until it's over, not too unlike riding the world's largest roller coaster. And how many people can stay perfectly silent once that roller coaster starts moving down the tracks?

No healthy birth takes place without noise—or without pain. I know this not only from my own childbearing years but also from studying human labor and birth from a wide variety of perspectives as a reproductive health specialist. Because I have become something of an expert on this subject, I have absolutely no qualms about using the word *pain* to describe labor. Like it or not, that's the word we use for noticeable physical discomfort or unpleasant bodily sensations.

Breathing, relaxation, attention, focus, massage, maternal positioning, and other coping techniques can significantly ease labor pain, but these measures don't normally erase it. What makes this amazing, arduous journey both bearable and also joyous isn't the Lamaze method. It's our love for our children and the anticipation of meeting and holding them when the process is finally over. The seemingly endless months of stretching, dreaming, praying, and hoping—the awesome, abiding awareness of mothering a brand-new life during pregnancy—contain deep purpose, value, and meaning. One of the hardest things about this period of anticipation is *waiting*—intimately sharing every moment of our existence with someone we already love but can't see, touch, or hear yet. By the time nine months go by, we're typically more than ready to give birth—

regardless of the effort required, in spite of whatever pain might be involved—because we dearly desire to greet our beloved children face to face.

> FOCUS POINT➢ Living with our heavenly destination in mind and honestly acknowledging the reality of pain in our world helps us fasten our thoughts and desires on Christ.

The world we live in is not as it once was and not as it will one day be. Our anxious waiting "for that day when God will give us our full rights as his children, including the new bodies he has promised us" is not a soundless, predictable, easy process. The "foretaste of future glory" we have received from the Holy Spirit, rather than eliminating our groaning hunger for Christ and His kingdom, significantly sharpens our longing.

"Suffering makes us want to go there. Broken homes and broken hearts crush our illusions that earth can keep its promises, that it can really satisfy," states Joni Eareckson Tada, who has lived most of her life in a wheelchair since being paralyzed in a diving accident. "Only the hope of heaven can truly move our passions off this world—which God knows could never fulfill us anyway—and place them where they will find their glorious fulfillment."[3] In spite of what popular trends, theories, and theology may tell us, just as there is no painless birth, there is no painless life.

Like pregnancy, life can seem strangely meaningless if we discount or dismiss its eternal purpose and value in the presence of painful, confusing contradictions. But when we stop, focus our eyes of

The desert initiates us into the life of the Spirit by helping us to discover who we most deeply are. . . . Christ asks us to abandon our idols, whatever they may be, and to love Him with our entire being.

ANDREW MURRAY

Dry wells send us to the fountain.

SAMUEL RUTHERFORD

Real pain can alone cure us of many ills.

JONATHAN EDWARDS

faith on Jesus, and quiet our hearts long enough to truly recognize and feel the discomfort, we find Christ waiting to meet us at the heart of our deep groaning.

"The many contradictions in our lives—such as being home while feeling homeless, being busy while feeling bored, being popular while feeling lonely, being believers while feeling many doubts—can frustrate, irritate, and even discourage us. Every door that opens for us makes us see how many more doors are closed," suggests Henri Nouwen. "But there is another response. These same contradictions can bring us into touch with a deeper longing for the fulfillment of a desire that lives beneath all desires and that only God can satisfy. Contradictions, thus understood, create the friction that can help move us toward God."[4]

Perhaps this is one of the reasons why the psalmists persisted always in singing God's praises in the face of life's most wrenching contradictions—songs of hope in praise of the Lord of life; prayers of the heart revealing every hue in the broad spectrum of human emotion; promises of thanksgiving interspersed with confessions of sin, suffering, and seemingly insurmountable struggle. These are the Psalms, the "prayer and praise songbook" of Scripture. Each refrain informs us that these singers understood about aiming their souls' hunger toward God, both in times of trial and celebration.

We can't find a better mirror than the Psalms in which to see our innermost thoughts and secret desires. The soaring words of this book of praise invite our active reply. No other passages in the Bible offer such vivid descriptions of worship in the midst of tribulation. No other book paints a clearer view of the interior landscape of praise and adoration. No other Scripture verses contain more convincing word pictures of what it means to find refuge, strength, and sustenance from God.

The Psalms show us how to sing as we labor, demonstrating that praise is a vital God-given coping strategy designed to lighten our loads, ease our weariness, change our perspective, refresh our spirits, and raise our hearts toward Home in preparation for the road ahead. More to the point, our sighs and groans are lifted as a fragrant sacrifice toward God's throne in heaven when we sing God's praises.

Does this mean we are to manufacture praise artificially or act as if we're happy when our hearts are breaking? Definitely not! It's possible to draw near to God in spirit and in truth *no matter how we feel*. That's exactly what David did. Whether he felt crushed or victorious, defeated or triumphant, cast down or exalted, David was ready to declare God's ability to sustain and deliver him. In his psalms we see over and over again that praise is a choice, not an emotion.

Consider Psalm 13, for example, where David cries out to the Lord for deliverance from a life-threatening illness. In spite of his physical weakness, David elects to trust in God's love and rejoice in the miracle of His salvation. With thanksgiving he closes the psalm in recognition of God's goodness, making a vow to praise his Creator in *anticipation* of answered prayer.

"I trust in your unfailing love," David sang (Ps. 13:5). Through his soaring psalms, David confirms that the music of our hearts matters to God, that His ear is tuned to the pitch and tone of our voices. Like David, we too can sing with honesty to the One who gives us eternal life and matchless love. He is a God we can trust with *any* problem—a King worthy of honor and praise who knows our every need.

"There are songs that can be learned only in the valley. No art can teach them; no rules of voice can make them perfectly sung. Their music is in the heart," stressed George Matheson, a blind Scottish pastor, in the nineteenth century. "And so, my soul, thou art receiving a music lesson from thy Father. Thou are being educated for the choir invisible.

The Lord will protect you from all evil; He will keep your soul. The Lord will guard your going out and your coming in from this time forth and forever.

PSALM 121:7-8 NASB

It is easy to forget that becoming a Christian is only the beginning. The journey of a thousand miles begins with the first step, but the purpose of this first step is the whole journey. It is not the other way around.

OS GUINNESS

There are parts of the symphony that none can take but thee. There are chords too minor for the angels. There are heights which angels alone can reach; but there are depths that belong to *thee*, and can only be touched by thee."[5]

Valley songs are the unique expression of hearts longing to ascend to the mountaintops. Joy awaits those who are willing to keep on climbing. When you sense you're approaching the end of your ability to cope, I urge you: Do your soul a favor and dine on the Psalms.

> FOCUS POINT➢ We were not designed to depend on human fantasies and ideals, but on God alone, as our soul's source of life, strength, shelter, and provision.

We were never meant to endure our earthly existence alone, in the dark, without hope and without help, on our journey toward eternity. Thankfully, we *aren't* alone. God has supernaturally provided us with a prayer partner, the Holy Spirit, who immeasurably aids and assist us: "And the Holy Spirit helps us in our distress. For we don't even know what we should pray for, nor how we should pray. But the Holy Spirit prays for us with groanings that cannot be expressed in words. And the Father who knows all hearts knows what the Spirit is saying, for the Spirit pleads for us believers in harmony with God's own will. And we know that God causes everything to work together for the good of those who love God and are called according to his purpose for them" (Rom. 8:26-28 NLT).

Once again Paul's words point us toward the intensity of the birth process. As any experienced labor partner will tell you, it's usually clear when an unmedicated expectant mother enters the active phase of labor because she no longer converses during contractions, but must consciously focus her complete attention on breathing and relaxation in order to cope. Neither can she monitor and evaluate her own progress; instead, she must rely on the support and strength of others.

Like a laboring woman caught up in working through her contractions, it's easy for us to lose perspective about why we're here and where we're going. Too often we make the mistake of relying on our stressed-out brains and finite strength when the Holy Spirit is already assisting us in our weakness—

helping us, interceding for us, pleading for us in harmony with God's will. What's more, our Advocate is groaning right along with us.

This is tremendously comforting. We have not only God's Word to fill and strengthen us but His Spirit to aid us day by day on our journey Home. As we encounter painful experiences in our fallen world, caught up in a birthing process we can't step out of until it's over, where will we choose to look for comfort, sustenance, and satisfaction? Substitutes, no matter what or who they are, will never satisfy us.

Savoring God's Word—continuously recollecting, musing, pondering, considering, reflecting on the truth—provides the strength we need to press forward with endurance. More than a coping strategy, reflecting on the Word with the Holy Spirit's help as we wait upon the Lord is a continuing privilege—and challenge—that richly feeds our souls. Repentance, obedience, faithfulness, and a deepened longing for God are the results.[6] In the Bible we find fifty-eight references to meditation. In every instance, Scripture emphasizes the transformed attitude that comes about as we hear God speak to us through His Word.

"Meditation is the activity of calling to mind, and thinking over, and dwelling on, and applying to oneself, the various things that one knows about the works and ways and purposes and promises of God," explains Dr. J. I. Packer, adding:

> It is an activity of holy thought, consciously performed in the presence of God, under the eye of God, by the help of God, as a means

Impossible as it may seem, it is the unusual privilege of the Christian to be aware of God at all times.

JOHN WHITE

You can set up an altar to God in your mind by means of prayer. And so it is fitting to pray at your trade, on a journey, standing at a counter, or sitting at your handcraft.

JOHN OF CHRYSOSTOM

The best way out is always through.

ROBERT FROST

> of communion with God. Its purpose is to clear one's mental and spiritual vision of God, and to let His truth make its full and proper impact on one's mind and heart. It is a matter of talking to God and oneself; it is, indeed, often a matter of arguing with oneself, reasoning oneself out of moods of doubt and unbelief into a clear apprehension of God's power and grace. Its effect is ever to humble us, as we contemplate God's greatness and glory, and our own littleness and sinfulness, and to encourage and reassure us—"comfort" us, in the old, strong, Bible sense of the word—as we contemplate the unsearchable riches of divine mercy displayed in the Lord Jesus Christ . . . . And it is as we enter more and more deeply into this experience of being humbled and exalted that our knowledge of God increases, and with it our peace, our strength, our joy.[7]

Contemplating the "unsearchable riches of divine mercy" provides us with an inexhaustible supply of truth and wonder with which to fill our thoughts. "True contentment is a real, even an active, virtue—not only affirmative but creative," affirmed the English author and essayist G. K. Chesterton. "It is the power of getting out of any situation what there is in it."[8]

Just as the birthing process requires a woman to cope with only one contraction at a time, the way of faith requires us to walk with the Lord one step at a time. We expectantly wait for him, not giving up in discouragement or frustration, not getting ahead of the Holy Spirit by going outside God's boundaries or trying to win His approval through performance.

Jesus tells us: "Give your entire attention to what God is doing right now, and don't get worked up about what may or may not happen tomorrow. God will help you deal with whatever hard things come up when the time comes" (Matt. 6:34 THE MESSAGE).

FOCUS POINT➢ Reach out for all God has for you! Don't be content with less.

"The God we must learn to know," A. W. Tozer reminds us, "is the Majesty of the heavens, the Father almighty, the Maker of heaven and earth, the only wise God our Savior."[9]

Jesus taught that prayer centers first on the Creator, not the created; on the supernatural rather than the natural; on our heavenly Father instead of on ourselves. "Our Father in heaven, hallowed be *your* name, *your* kingdom come, *your* will be done on earth as it is in heaven," He prayed (Matt. 6:9-10). It is from this vantage point that we pray as we honor and recognize the everlasting source of our help, strength, nurture, and protection.

In a very real sense, prayer opens our eyes to the state of God's groaning creation. Through prayer we acknowledge who we are before the Lord and seek to know His will. Like the psalmist, we lift our eyes "to the hills" in order to fix our attention on the direction our Father wants us to go, alerting us to the unseen realms of God. This type of spiritual alertness is never an automatic reaction, especially when multiple distractions and earthbound appetites pull our thoughts back down on a regular basis.

In his letter to the Ephesians, Paul uses such words as *plead*, *remind*, and *earnest* in regard to prayer, even admonishing believers to "pray at all times and on every occasion in the power of the Holy Spirit" (Eph. 6:18 NLT). Praying this way requires attentiveness, profound dependence on the Holy Spirit, and a continuing desire to look beyond the idols of this world to the eternal realities of God's kingdom. Through a mind-numbing, pervasive barrage of self-help messages, seductive images, and mood music, it's difficult to feel the urgency Paul did. But when our labor pangs intensify, when we are moved by the groanings of others, when we weep with compassion and

There are a lot of things that only happen once. Remembering that simple fact will help us live through them.

Jill Briscoe

We cannot get away from God, but we can ignore Him.

William Allen Butler

Prayer is the determination to be alone before God, with no gallery to play to and no distracting comparisons to make.

James Houston

concern for the suffering we witness throughout God's creation, we awake and realize that drawing near the Lord through prayer is our best response.

In his classic book, *How to Pray*, R. A. Torrey wrote that to be effective, prayer "should really be *unto* God . . . a definite and conscious approach to God . . . a definite and conscious realization that God is bending over us as we pray." Torrey continued:

> In very much of our prayer there is really but little thought of God. Our mind is taken up with the thought of what we need, and is not occupied with the thought of the mighty and loving Father of whom we are seeking it.
>
> Oftentimes . . . we are occupied neither with the need nor with the One to whom we are praying, but our mind is wandering here and there throughout the world. But when we really come into God's presence, really meet Him face to face in the place of prayer, really seek the things we desire *from Him*, then there is power.[10]

Hunger for the Lord and the reality of His kingdom lies at the root of all effective prayer. Though our minds and hearts are easily distracted from this pursuit, the Holy Spirit helps us in our weakness. Our part is to be attentive, watchful, ready, and obedient to turn our thoughts toward the thoughts of God. Praying in accord with the Holy Spirit depends primarily upon our eagerness and willingness to participate in prayer and cannot—must not—rely on mere "head knowledge" alone. Because the Holy Spirit helps us and intercedes for us, we can be confident that our prayers are effective and powerful.

"As the Spirit breathes out the 'Father' cry of a child, which is the prayer-cry, so he helps us in our praying," S. D. Gordon points out. "He is the master-prayer. He knows God's will perfectly. He knows what's best to be praying in all circumstances. And He is within you and me . . . . He prompts us to pray. He calls us to the quiet room to our knees. He inclines us to prayer wherever we are."[11]

As you wait upon the Lord to prepare your heart for prayer, ask Him for the strength of focused concentration. Pull your thoughts back from daydreaming, fixing your attention on a brief portion of God's Word. For example: "Search me, O God, and know my heart; test me and know my anxious thoughts," might be a helpful starting point (Ps. 139:23). Wait on the Lord—on His presence, on His cleansing. Worship Him with reverence and awe. Taste and see the goodness of your Maker. Then prayer will become a cooperative endeavor and a time of rich blessing as the Holy Spirit enables you to pray effectively, articulately, and with heartfelt desire and compassion.

"The greatest prayer anyone can offer is, 'Thy will be done.' It will be offered in a thousand different forms, with a thousand different details, as needs arise daily. But every true prayer comes from those words," stated Gordon. But, he cautions, "There might be a false submission to His supposed will in some affliction; a not reaching out for *all* He has for us."[12]

Given the scope of prayer—what prayer throughout the ages has accomplished—we have every reason to "approach the throne of grace with confidence, so that we may receive mercy and find grace to help us in our time of need" (Heb. 4:16).

"Our first prayer needs simply to tell God, 'O God, help me to pray, because I cannot pray by myself,'" Dr. James Houston reminds us. "Such a prayer helps us recognize how prayer expresses our deepest need before the kingship of God."[13]

Prayer is the vehicle we use to leave the heart's heavy loads at the foot of the cross. In prayer we turn to face God as we are, with longing, hunger, and thirst, asking to be filled again. Prayer is the

When the flesh is satisfied, it is hard to pray with cheerfulness or to devote oneself to a life of service which calls for much self-renunciation.

DIETRICH BONHOEFFER

If you're still anticipating something you are asking God to do in your life, don't try to manipulate Him or your circumstances. Let Him bring it about and be prepared to keep trusting Him if it doesn't happen.

TONY EVANS

entry point into the practice of patience, the means by which we surrender our burdens, accept our limitations, see the next step, and receive spiritual sustenance as we continue on in God's strength rather than our own. Through prayer we find the strength to be quiet as we wait. Through prayer we learn the secret of being content in Christ. "Prayer," discerned John Bunyan in the seventeenth century, "opens the heart to God, and it is the means by which the soul, though empty, is filled by God."[14]

With each passing hour, we're growing closer to the moment when we will finally greet Jesus face to face. We don't know how long it will take us to reach our destination. Sometimes it seems we may never get there, that we'll always be caught up in this state of groaning, that we will never see the Lord's smile, touch His hand, or hear His voice.

When we're caught up in the pressing demands of life's labor and tempted to forget who we are, where we're going, why we're still hungry for *more*, may we often remember this trustworthy passage: "And even we Christians, although we have the Holy Spirit within us as a foretaste of future glory, also groan to be released from pain and suffering. We, too, wait anxiously for that day when God will give us our full rights as his children, including the new bodies he has promised us. Now that we are saved, we eagerly look forward to this freedom. For if you already have something, you don't need to hope for it. But if we look forward to something we don't have yet, we must wait patiently and confidently" (Rom. 8:23-25 NLT).

With these words the truth is made plain: We will not gain full satisfaction this side of heaven. Yes, we've been given an appetizing sample of the glorious things to come, but we're still waiting for our dinner. We haven't been seated at the King's banquet table just yet. In a little while, in a little while . . . .

In the meantime, we groan for release and relief—waiting anxiously, eagerly looking forward to, and needing to hope for something we don't already have. No matter where we find ourselves along our homeward journey today, through praise and worship, meditation on God's Word, and prayer, we learn to be content while remaining less than fully satisfied, resting in the knowledge that our continuing hunger pangs direct our appetite toward God's promised feast.

Jesus! The very thought of Thee
With sweetness fills my breast;
But sweeter far Thy face to see,
And in Thy presence rest.

No voice can sing, nor heart can frame
Nor can the mem'ry find
A sweeter sound than Thy blest name,
O Savior of mankind!

O hope of ev'ry contrite heart,
O Joy of all the meek,
To those who fall, how kind Thou art!
How good to those who seek!

But what to those who find? Ah! this
Nor tongue nor pen can show—
The love of Jesus, what it is,
None but His loved ones know.

Jesus, our only joy be Thou,
As Thou our prize wilt be;
In Thee be all our glory now
And through eternity.

—BERNARD OF CLAIRVAUX

FOCUS POINTS

➢ Living with our heavenly destination in mind and honestly acknowledging the reality of pain in our world helps us fasten our thoughts and desires on Christ.

➢ We were not designed to depend on human fantasies and ideals, but on God alone, as our soul's source of life, strength, shelter, and provision.

➢ Reach out for all God has for you! Don't be content with less.

Nourishment from God's Word

The Lord is my shepherd; I have everything I need.
He lets me rest in green meadows; he leads me beside peaceful streams.
He renews my strength.
He guides me along right paths, bringing honor to his name.
Even when I walk through the dark valley of death,
I will not be afraid, for you are close beside me.
Your rod and your staff protect and comfort me.
You prepare a feast for me in the presence of my enemies.
You welcome me as a guest, anointing my head with oil.
My cup overflows with blessings.
Surely your goodness and unfailing love will pursue me
all the days of my life, and I will dwell in the house of the LORD *forever.*

—PSALM 23 NLT

Yes, the Sovereign LORD *is coming in all his glorious power. He will rule with awesome strength. See, he brings his reward with him as he comes. He will feed his flock like a shepherd. He will carry the lambs in his arms, holding them close to his heart. He will gently lead the mother sheep with their young.*

—ISAIAH 40:10-11 NLT

Some of his disciples said to one another, "What does he mean by saying, 'In a little while you will see me no more, and then after a little while you will see me,' and 'Because I am going to the Father'?" They kept asking, "What does he mean by 'a little while'? We don't understand what he is saying."

Jesus saw that they wanted to ask him about this, so he said to them, "Are you asking one another what I meant when I said, 'In a little while you will see me no more, and then after a little while you will see me'? I tell you the truth, you will weep and mourn while the world rejoices. You will grieve, but your grief will turn to joy. A woman giving birth to a child has pain because her time has come; but when her baby is born she forgets the anguish because of her joy that a child is born into the world. So with you: Now is your time of grief, but I will see you again and you will rejoice, and no one will take away your joy."

—JOHN 16:17-22

No wonder we do not lose heart! Though our outward humanity is in decay, yet day by day we are inwardly renewed. Our troubles are slight and short-lived; and their outcome an eternal glory which outweighs them far. Meanwhile our eyes are fixed, not on the things that are seen, but on the things that are unseen: for what is seen passes away; what is unseen is eternal.

For we know that if the earthly frame that houses us today should be demolished, we possess a building which God has provided—a house not made by human hands, eternal, and in heaven. In this present body we do indeed groan; we yearn to have our heavenly habitation put on over this one—in the hope that, being thus clothed, we shall not find ourselves naked. We groan indeed, we who are enclosed within this earthly frame; we are oppressed because we do not want to have the old body stripped off. Rather our desire is to have the new body put on over it, so that our mortal part may be absorbed into life immortal. God himself has shaped us for this very end; and as a pledge of it he has given us the Spirit.

Therefore we never cease to be confident. We know that so long as we are at home in the body we are exiles from the Lord; faith is our guide, we do not see him. We are confident, I repeat, and would rather leave our home in the body and go to live with the Lord. We therefore make it our ambition, wherever we are, here or there, to be acceptable to him. For we must all have our lives laid open before the tribunal of Christ, where each must receive what is due to him for his conduct in the body, good or bad.

—2 CORINTHIANS 4:16-18; 5:1-10 NEB

Reflection Points

1. Like prayer, praise is a privilege to be practiced with . . . .
2. In times of sorrow or crisis I've discovered praise can be a comfort if . . . .
3. The greatest hindrance to my personal communion with God is . . . .
4. To avoid being distracted as I quietly reflect on God's Word, I . . . .
5. I'm most encouraged to pray when . . . .
6. The more I pray, the more I learn about . . . .
7. I think praise is portrayed in the Bible as a sacrifice because . . . .

Additional Study

—*MEDITATE ON* Psalms 8; 30; 91; 95; 98; 100; 102; 103.

—*READ ABOUT* three biblical women persistently cooperating with God's plans and purposes:

The *Shunammite woman*, Elisha's hostess sustained by firm faith, 2 Kings 4:8-37; 8:1-6.

Hannah, who, by pouring out her pain in prayer, found God's strong comfort and consolation, in 1 Samuel 1:1—2:11; 2:19-21.

Mary and Elizabeth, two cousins filled with praise and joy, Luke 1:39-56.

—*STUDY* Psalm 18:25-36; Psalm 66:8-20; John 6:52-59; John 14:1-35; John 16:5-16; 1 Corinthians 15:35-58; Ephesians 1:3-23; Colossians 1:9-23; 1 Thessalonians 4:13-18; Philippians 2:1-13; Revelation 19:6-9.

—*MEMORIZE* Joshua 1:5; Psalm 16:7-8; Psalm 121:1-2; Psalm 141:1-2; Proverbs 8:17; Isaiah 41:10; Jeremiah 29:13; Matthew 26:41; Luke 11:10; John 6:54; 2 Corinthians 1:3; Hebrews 12:2; 1 Timothy 6:6; Hebrews 13:15; James 5:7-8; 1 John 5:14; Jude 1:21; Revelation 22:12-13.

Suggested Exercises

- When you are immersed in the stressful here and now of your journey toward heaven, being thankful will help you to recognize and remember the things God has already done. Giving thanks allows your soul to sing, especially on down days when praising God may be the *last* thing on your personal agenda. "That my soul may sing praise to You and not be silent. O LORD my God, I will give thanks to You forever" (Ps. 30:12 NASB).
- One means of sharpening your awareness of the Lord's attentive love for you is recalling His custom-made blessings. As you thank Him for what He has done, you develop the habit of gratitude and expand your trust in His present mercy. To discourage forgetfulness on difficult days, keep a Remembrance Box. Stock it with mementoes of God's personalized provision for you—letters, ticket stubs, cards, fabric scraps, receipts, Bible verses, notes, photos, dried flowers, lists, rocks (you name it). You may also want to purchase or make a Reminder Book to keep on hand for the same pur-

pose, filling it with anything that jogs your memory of surprise blessings and answered prayers.

- Prayer always is your best response as you seek God's wisdom, help, and strength in every situation. Using this short scriptural summary, look up the verses cited below and with your own insights and observations explain how prayer has worked on your behalf in each area. Feel free to enhance this list with as many additional themes and verses as you like.

Prayer recognizes that God is in control (Ps. 31:15):

Prayer promotes peace (Phil. 4:6-7):

Prayer partners with thanksgiving (1 Thess. 5:16-18):

Prayer eases the burden (Matt. 11:28):

Prayer brings protection from harm (Ps. 32:6):

Prayer defeats the opposition (Eph. 6:10-18):

Prayer builds spiritual strength (Col. 1:9-12):

Prayer provides wisdom (James 1:5):

Prayer puts our love for others into action (Phil. 1:9-11):

Prayer goes where we can't go and does what we can't do (Rom. 8:26-27):

• Reflect on the following passage. Then write Paul's words in your notebook, separating and highlighting the lines for personal emphasis. After noting which of the short segments affected you most deeply, for about five to ten minutes meditate on these words only. Spend some time journaling your impressions.

> *All I care for is to know Christ, to experience the power of his resurrection, and to share his sufferings, in growing conformity with his death, if only I may finally arrive at the resurrection from the dead. It is not to be thought that I have already achieved all this. I have not yet reached perfection, but I press on, hoping to take hold of that for which Christ once took hold of me. My friends, I do not reckon myself to have got hold of it yet. All I can say is this: forgetting what is behind me, and reaching out for that which lies ahead, I press towards the goal to win the prize which is God's call to the life above, in Christ Jesus. (Philippians 3:10-14* NEB*)*

Closing Prayer

O Lord God, our Governor, we beseech Thee, of Thy mercy, that we may have the heavenly vision, and behold things as they seem to Thee, that the turmoil of this world may be seen by us to be bringing forth the sweet peace of the eternal years, and that in all the troubles and sorrows of our own hearts we may behold good, and so, with quiet mind and inward peace, careless of outward storm, we may do the duty of life which brings us a quiet heart, ever trusting in Thee. We give Thee thanks for all Thy mercy. We beseech Thy forgiveness for our sins. We pray Thy guidance in all things, Thy presence in the hour of our death, Thy glory in the life to come. Of Thy mercy, hear us, through Jesus Christ our Lord — Amen.[15]

—GEORGE DAWSON
(1821-1870)

May the God of all grace, who called us to His eternal glory by Christ Jesus, after you have suffered a while, perfect, establish, strengthen, and settle you. To Him be the glory and the dominion forever and ever. Amen. (1 Peter 5:10-11 NKJV)

FOOD FOR THOUGHT

Brief life here is our portion;
Brief sorrow, short-lived care;
The life that knows no ending,
The tearless life, is there.

O happy retribution
Short toil, eternal rest:
For mortals and for sinners
A mansion with the blest.

And now we fight the battle,
But then shall wear the crown
Of full and everlasting
And passionless renown.

And now we watch and struggle,
And now we live in hope,
And Sion in her anguish
With Babylon must cope.

But He whom now we trust in
Shall then be seen and known;
And they that know and see Him
Shall have Him for their own.

The morning shall awaken,
The shadows flee away,
And each true-hearted servant
Shall shine as doth the day.

There God, our King and Patron,
In fullness of His grace,
Shall we behold forever
And worship face to face.[16]

—BERNARD OF CLAIRVAUX

Notes

Introduction

1. Oswald Chambers, *My Utmost for His Highest* (New York: Dodd, Mead, 1935), 350.
2. Sheila Cragg, quoted in *Beyond Today* (Wheaton, Ill.: Crossway Books, 2000), 85.
3. Christina Rossetti, *Goblin Market and Other Poems* (London: Macmillan, 1862), 130-131.

Chapter One: The Hunger We Have

1. Augustine of Hippo, quoted in *The Joy of the Saints*, ed. Robert Llewelyn (Springfield, Ill.: Templegate, 1988), 1.
2. Philip James Bailey, quoted in *12,000 Religious Quotations*, ed. Frank S. Mead (Grand Rapids: Baker, 1989), 166.
3. Dallas Willard, *The Divine Conspiracy: Rediscovering Our Hidden Life in God* (San Francisco: HarperSanFrancisco, 1998), 271, 272.
4. Richard Blanchard, "Fill My Cup, Lord," in *The Hymnal for Worship & Celebration* (Waco, Tex.: Word Music, 1986), 398.
5. Excerpts taken from "Reality," by Frances Ridley Havergal, in *The World's Great Religious Poetry* (New York: Macmillan, 1923), 325-327.
6. Samuel Osgood, quoted in *Prayers: Ancient and Modern*, comp. Mary Wilder Tileston (New York: Grosset & Dunlap, 1897), 359.
7. George Macdonald, *Donal Grant* (Boston: D. Lothrop, 1883), 79-80.

Chapter Two: The Junk Food We Eat

1. Phillips Brooks, quoted in *Disciplines for the Inner Life*, ed. Bob Benson and Michael W. Benson (Nashville: Thomas Nelson, 1989), 286.
2. Max Lucado, *Grace for the Moment* (Nashville: J. Countryman, 2000), 25.
3. Anne Morrow Lindbergh, *Gift from the Sea* (New York: Pantheon, 1955), 52.
4. Francis Quarles, from "Delight in God Only," *Lyra Anglicana* (New York: D. Appleton, 1865), 12.
5. M. F. K. Fisher, *The Art of Eating* (Cleveland: World Publishing, 1954), 10-11.
6. R. C. Sproul, *The Soul's Quest for God* (Wheaton, Ill.: Tyndale, 1992), 17.
7. Ibid., 6.

8. Bernard of Clairvaux, *The Love of God*, ed. James M. Houston (Portland, Ore.: Multnomah, 1983), 149-151.
9. Augustine of Hippo, quoted in *Prayers: Ancient and Modern*, comp. Mary Wilder Tileston (New York: Grosset & Dunlap, 1897), 142. Feminine pronouns have been added.
10. Edith Schaeffer, *A Way of Seeing* (Old Tappan, N.J.: Fleming H. Revell, 1977), 248-250.

Chapter Three: The Shape of Our Appetites

1. Martin Luther, quoted in *The Joy of the Saints*, ed. Robert L. Llewelyn (Springfield, Ill.: Templegate, 1988), 72.
2. Ibid., 66.
3. Dick Keyes, *Beyond Identity* (Ann Arbor, Mich.: Servant, 1984), 133.
4. Ibid., 133, 102.
5. Blaise Pascal, quoted in John Bartlett, *Bartlett's Familiar Quotations,* 16th ed., ed. Justin Kaplan (Boston: Little, Brown and Company, 1992), 270.
6. Hannah Whitall Smith, *The Christian's Secret of a Happy Life* (Westwood, N.J.: Spire/Fleming H. Revell, 1970), 92.
7. Ibid., 92-93.
8. James Houston, *The Heart's Desire* (Colorado Springs: NavPress, 1996), 7.
9. Keyes, *Beyond Identity*, 107.
10. Dietrich Bonhoeffer, *The Cost of Discipleship* (New York: Macmillan, 1963), 47-48.
11. Anne Bradstreet, "The Vanity of All Worldly Things," in *The Works of Anne Bradstreet*, ed. John Harvard Ellis (Charleston, S. C.: A. E. Cutter, 1867).
12. Thomas Aquinas, quoted in *Prayers: Ancient and Modern*, comp. Mary Wilder Tileston (New York: Grosset & Dunlap, 1897), 42.
13. Hannah More, *The Works of Hannah More, Vol. 1* (New York: Harper & Brothers, 1841), 440-442.

Chapter Four: The Promise of a Spiritual Makeover

1. Hannah More, *Practical Piety* (New York: Appleton, 1854), 14.
2. Roberta Pollack Seid, *Never Too Thin: Why Women Are at War with Their Bodies* (New York: Prentice Hall, 1989), 3.
3. Ibid., 4.
4. Lori Miller Case, "The Weight Game," *Bazaar*, April 1993, 291.
5. Nanci Hellmich, "Innovative Fat-Fighter Jean Nidetch," *USA Today*, May 18, 1993, 1D.

6. J. I. Packer, *Knowing God* (Downers Grove, Ill.: InterVarsity, 1973), 185.
7. John White, *The Fight* (Downers Grove, Ill.: InterVarsity, 1976), 13.
8. Ibid., 13-15.
9. Eugene H. Peterson, *A Long Obedience in the Same Direction* (Downers Grove, Ill.: InterVarsity, 1980), 21.
10. Ibid., 25-26.
11. Francis Schaeffer, *True Spirituality* (Wheaton, Ill.: Tyndale, 1971), 43.
12. Charles Colson, *Loving God* (Grand Rapids: Zondervan, 1983), 25.
13. Oswald Chambers, *My Utmost for His Highest* (New York: Dodd, Mead, 1935), 227.
14. More, *Practical Piety*, 16.
15. Emily Dickinson, LXXVI, *The Poems of Emily Dickinson*(Boston: Little, Brown and Company, 1924), 36.
16. Bernard of Clairvaux, quoted in *His Victorious Dwelling*, ed. Nick Harrison (Grand Rapids: Zondervan, 1998), 62-63.
17. Anselm of Canterbury, quoted in *Prayers: Ancient and Modern*, comp. Mary Wilder Tileston (New York: Grosset & Dunlap, 1897), 120.
18. C. S. Lewis, *Mere Christianity* (New York: Macmillan, 1952), 190.

Chapter 5: The Joy and Passion of Waiting on God

1. Oswald Chambers, *My Utmost for His Highest* (New York: Dodd, Mead, 1935), 73.
2. Dick Keyes, *Beyond Identity* (Ann Arbor, Mich.: Servant, 1984), 99.
3. Ibid., 84.
4. Hannah Whitall Smith, *The Christian's Secret of a Happy Life* (Westwood, N.J.: Spire/Fleming H. Revell, 1970), 126. Italics mine.
5. Edward W. Goodrick and John R. Kohlenberger III, eds., James A. Swanson, assoc. ed., *Zondervan Exhaustive Concordance* (Grand Rapids: Zondervan, 1999), #7747.
6. Dietrich Bonhoeffer, *Life Together* (New York: Harper & Brothers, 1954), 80.
7. Henri J. M. Nouwen, *Making All Things New: An Invitation to the Spiritual Life* (New York: Harper & Row, 1981), 66.
8. Ibid., 67-68.
9. Chambers, *My Utmost for His Highest*, 8.
10. George T. Rider, ed., *Lyra Anglicana* (New York: D. Appleton, 1865), 210-211.
11. Jeremy Taylor, quoted in *Prayers: Ancient and Modern,* comp. Mary Wilder Tileston (New York: Grosset & Dunlap, 1897), 340.
12. Ibid.

13. C. H. Spurgeon, *The Treasury of David*, Vol. 2 (London: Passmore and Alabaster, 1871), 2-3.

Chapter 6: Face to Face

1. Fra Angelico, quoted in Margaret Carlson, *Grace Grows Best in Winter* (Grand Rapids: Eerdmans, 1984), 191-192.
2. John Harris, quoted in *His Victorious Dwelling*, ed. Nick Harrison (Grand Rapids: Zondervan, 1998), 175.
3. Joni Eareckson Tada, *Heaven: Your Real Home* (Grand Rapids: Zondervan, 1995), 182.
4. Henri Nouwen, *Bread for the Journey: A Daybook of Wisdom and Faith* (San Francisco: HarperSanFrancisco, 1997), April 20.
5. George Matheson, quoted in *My Heart Sings*, comp. Joan Winmill Brown (Waco, TX: Word, 1987), 150.
6. This idea is from Richard Foster, *Treasury of Christian Discipline* (New York: HarperCollins, 1988), 15.
7. J. I. Packer, *Knowing God* (Downers Grove, Ill.: InterVarsity, 1973), 18-19.
8. G. K. Chesterton, *The Doubleday Christian Quotation Collection,* comp. Hannah Ward and Jennifer Wild (New York: Doubleday, 1998), 208.
9. A. W. Tozer, *The Knowledge of the Holy* (New York: Harper & Row, 1961), 121.
10. R. A. Torrey, *How to Pray* (Old Tappan, N.J.: Fleming H. Revell, 1900).
11. S. D. Gordon, *Quiet Talks on Prayer* (Westwood, N.J.: The Christian Library, 1984).
12. Ibid.
13. James Houston, *The Transforming Power of Prayer* (Colorado Springs: NavPress, 1996), 78.
14. John Bunyan, quoted in *The New Encyclopedia of Christian Quotations,* comp. Mark Water (Grand Rapids: Baker, 2000), 757.
15. George Dawson, quoted in *Prayers: Ancient and Modern,* comp. Mary Wilder Tileston (New York: Grosset & Dunlap, 1897), 299.
16. Bernard of Clairvaux, "Jerusalem That Is Above: Part I," in *Lyra Anglicana* (New York: D. Appleton, 1865).

BIBLIOGRAPHY: RESOURCES AND READINGS

12, 000 Religious Quotations. Frank S. Mead, ed. Grand Rapids: Baker, 1989.

A Bright Tomorrow. Wheaton, Ill.: Crossway, 2001.

Allender, Dan B. and Tremper Longman, III. *The Cry of the Soul: How Our Emotions Reveal Our Deepest Questions About God*. Colorado Springs: NavPress, 1999.

Allender, Dan. *Bold Love*. Colorado Springs: NavPress, 1992.

Anderson, Neil T. *The Bondage Breaker*. Eugene, Ore.: Harvest House, 1990.

Andrewes, Lancelot. *The Private Devotions of Lancelot Andrewes*. John Henry Newman, trans. New York: Abingdon-Cokesbury, 1950.

Anselm of Canterbury. *The Prayers and Meditations of St. Anselm*. Benedicta Ward, trans. New York: Penguin Classics, 1973.

At Jesus' Feet. Edward W. Schramm, ed. Minneapolis: Augsburg, 1936.

Auden, W. H. *Selected Poetry of W. H. Auden*. New York: Modern Library, 1958.

Augustine of Hippo. *Daily Readings with St. Augustine*. Maura Sée, ed. Springfield, Ill.: Templegate, 1986.

_____. *The Confessions of St. Augustine*. Edward B. Pusey, trans. New York: Pocket, 1951.

Baillie, John. *A Diary of Private Prayer*. New York: Charles Scribner's Sons, 1949.

Bartlett's Familiar Quotations, 16th ed. Justin Kaplan, ed. Boston: Little, Brown and Company, 1992.

Barzun, Jacques. *From Dawn to Decadence*. New York: HarperCollins, 2000.

Bede. *A History of the English Church and People*. London: Penguin Classics, 1955.

Bell, Rudolph M. *Holy Anorexia*. Chicago: University of Chicago, 1985.

Bernanos, George. *The Diary of a Country Priest*. Pamela Morris, trans. New York: Image/Doubleday, 1954.

Bernard of Clairvaux. *The Love of God*. James M. Houston, ed. Portland, Ore.: Multnomah, 1983.

Bethge, Eberhard. *Dietrich Bonhoeffer: Man of Vision, Man of Courage*. New York: Harper & Row, 1979.

Between Heaven and Earth. Ken Gire, comp. San Francisco: HarperSanFrancisco, 1997.

Beyond Today. Wheaton, Ill.: Crossway, 2000.

Blackaby, Henry T. *Experiencing God: How to Live the Full Adventure of Knowing and Doing the Will of God*. Nashville: Broadman & Holman, 1998.

Blackaby, Henry T. and Claude V. King. *Experiencing God: Knowing and Doing His Will*. Nashville: Lifeway, 1990.

Blake, William. *Poems of William Blake*. William Butler Yeats, ed. New York: Modern Library, n.d.

Bloesch, Donald. *The Struggle of Prayer*. San Francisco: Harper & Row, 1980.

Blumberg, Joan Jacobs. *Fasting Girls: The Emergence of Anorexia Nervosa as a Modern Disease*. Cambridge, Mass.: Harvard University, 1988.

Bonhoeffer, Dietrich. *A Testament to Freedom*. San Francisco: HarperSanFrancisco, 1995.

_____. *Christ the Center*. New York: Harper & Row, 1960.

_____. *Creation and Fall/Temptation: Two Biblical Studies*. New York: Macmillan, 1959.

_____. *The Cost of Discipleship*. New York: Macmillan, 1959.

_____. *Dietrich Bonhoeffer: Selections from His Writings*. Aileen Taylor, ed. Springfield, Ill.: Templegate, 1992.

_____. *Letters and Papers from Prison*. New York: Macmillan, 1971.

_____. *Life Together.* New York: Harper & Brothers, 1954.

_____. *The Martyred Christian*. Joan Winmill Brown, ed. New York: Macmillan, 1983.

_____. *The Mystery of Holy Night*. New York: Crossroad, 1996.

_____. *Psalms: The Prayer Book of the Bible*. Minneapolis: Augsburg, 1970.

_____. *Sanctorum Communio*. London: Collins, 1963.

_____. *Spiritual Care*. Jay C. Rochelle, ed. Philadelphia: Fortress, 1985.

The Book of Common Prayer. New York: The Church Pension Fund, 1945.

Bosanquet, Mary. *The Life and Death of Dietrich Bonhoeffer*. London: Hodder and Stoughton, 1968.

Bounds, E. M. *The Necessity of Prayer.* Grand Rapids: Baker, 1976.

Bradstreet, Anne. "The Vanity of All Worldly Things," in *The Works of Anne Bradstreet*. John Harvard Ellis, ed. Charleston, S. C.: A. E. Cutter, 1867.

Brand, Paul and Philip Yancey. *Fearfully and Wonderfully Made*. Grand Rapids: Zondervan, 1980.

_____. *In His Image*. Grand Rapids: Zondervan, 1984.

Breakfast for the Soul. Judith Couchman, comp. Tulsa: Honor, 1998.

Bridges, Jerry. *The Pursuit of Holiness*. Colorado Springs: NavPress, 1978.

_____. *Trusting God*. Colorado Springs: NavPress, 1988.

Briscoe, Jill. *The One Year Book of Quiet Times with God*. Wheaton, Ill.: Tyndale, 1997.

_____. *Out of the Shelter in Storm and into God's Arms: Shelter in Turbulent Times*. Colorado Springs: Shaw/Waterbrook, 2000.

_____. *Prayer That Works*. Wheaton, Ill.: Tyndale, 2000.

_____. *Songs from Heaven and Earth*. Nashville: Thomas Nelson, 1985.

_____. *Women Who Changed Their World*. Wheaton, Ill.: Victor, 1991.

Brother Lawrence. *The Practice of the Presence of God*. Springdale, Penn.: Whitaker, 1982.

Brown, R. LaMon. *Growing Spiritually with the Saints: Catherine of Genoa and William Law*. Macon, Ga.: Peake Road, 1996.

Buechner, Frederick. *Telling Secrets*. New York: HarperCollins, 1991.

Bunyan, John. *The Pilgrim's Progress.* Cincinnati: Jennings and Graham, 1903.

Butler's Lives of the Saints. Michael Walsh, ed. San Francisco: HarperSanFrancisco, 1991.

Cahill, Thomas. *Desire of the Everlasting Hills*. New York: Nan A. Talese/Doubleday, 1999.

_____. *The Gift of the Jews*. New York: Nan A. Talese/Doubleday, 1998.

_____. *How the Irish Saved Civilization*. New York: Anchor/Doubleday, 1995.

Carlson, Margaret. *Grace Grows Best in Winter*. Grand Rapids: Eerdmans, 1984.

Carmichael, Amy. *Candles in the Dark*. Fort Washington, Penn.: Christian Literature Crusade, 1981.

_____. *Edges of His Ways*. Fort Washington, Penn.: Christian Literature Crusade, 1955.

_____. *Gold by Moonlight*. Fort Washington, Penn.: Christian Literature Crusade, 1992.

_____. *His Thoughts Said . . . His Father Said . . .* Fort Washington, Penn.: Christian Literature Crusade, 1941.

_____. *If*. Fort Washington, Penn.: Christian Literature Crusade, 1992.

_____. *Learning from God*. Stuart and Brenda Blance, eds. Fort Washington, Penn.: Christian Literature Crusade, 1985.

_____. *Mountain Breezes*. Fort Washington, Penn.: Christian Literature Crusade, 1999.

_____. *Rose from Brier*. Fort Washington, Penn.: Christian Literature Crusade, 1980.

_____. *Wings*. London: S.P.C.K., 1960.

Carter, Jimmy. *Living Faith*. New York: Times/Random House, 1996.

_____. *Sources of Strength*. New York: Times/Random House, 1997.

Case, Lori Miller. "The Weight Game," *Bazaar*, April 1993, 291.

Chambers, Oswald. *Daily Thoughts for Disciples*. Grand Rapids: Discovery House, 1994.

_____. *My Utmost for His Highest.* New York: Dodd, Mead, 1963.

The Charismatica: The Holy Spirit in the Bible. Richard A. Rosemeyer, ed. Chicago: Christianica Center, 1979.

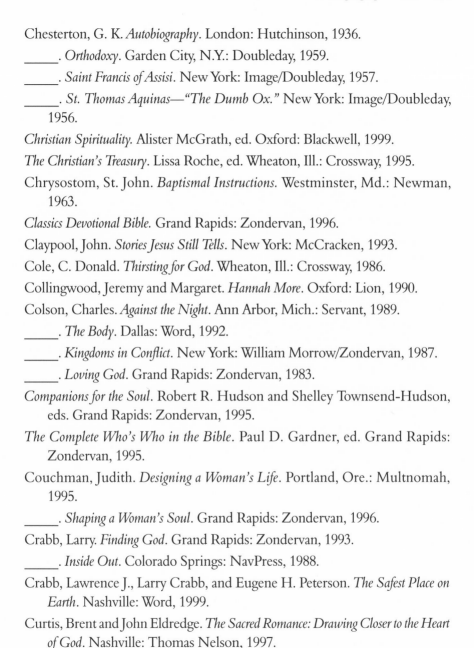

Chesterton, G. K. *Autobiography*. London: Hutchinson, 1936.

_____. *Orthodoxy*. Garden City, N.Y.: Doubleday, 1959.

_____. *Saint Francis of Assisi*. New York: Image/Doubleday, 1957.

_____. *St. Thomas Aquinas—"The Dumb Ox."* New York: Image/Doubleday, 1956.

Christian Spirituality. Alister McGrath, ed. Oxford: Blackwell, 1999.

The Christian's Treasury. Lissa Roche, ed. Wheaton, Ill.: Crossway, 1995.

Chrysostom, St. John. *Baptismal Instructions*. Westminster, Md.: Newman, 1963.

Classics Devotional Bible. Grand Rapids: Zondervan, 1996.

Claypool, John. *Stories Jesus Still Tells*. New York: McCracken, 1993.

Cole, C. Donald. *Thirsting for God*. Wheaton, Ill.: Crossway, 1986.

Collingwood, Jeremy and Margaret. *Hannah More*. Oxford: Lion, 1990.

Colson, Charles. *Against the Night*. Ann Arbor, Mich.: Servant, 1989.

_____. *The Body*. Dallas: Word, 1992.

_____. *Kingdoms in Conflict*. New York: William Morrow/Zondervan, 1987.

_____. *Loving God*. Grand Rapids: Zondervan, 1983.

Companions for the Soul. Robert R. Hudson and Shelley Townsend-Hudson, eds. Grand Rapids: Zondervan, 1995.

The Complete Who's Who in the Bible. Paul D. Gardner, ed. Grand Rapids: Zondervan, 1995.

Couchman, Judith. *Designing a Woman's Life*. Portland, Ore.: Multnomah, 1995.

_____. *Shaping a Woman's Soul*. Grand Rapids: Zondervan, 1996.

Crabb, Larry. *Finding God*. Grand Rapids: Zondervan, 1993.

_____. *Inside Out*. Colorado Springs: NavPress, 1988.

Crabb, Lawrence J., Larry Crabb, and Eugene H. Peterson. *The Safest Place on Earth*. Nashville: Word, 1999.

Curtis, Brent and John Eldredge. *The Sacred Romance: Drawing Closer to the Heart of God*. Nashville: Thomas Nelson, 1997.

de Caussade, Jean-Pierre. *The Flame of Divine Love*. Robert Llewelyn, ed. London: Darton, Longman and Todd, 1984.

_____. *The Joy of Full Surrender*. Hal M. Helms, ed. Orleans, Mass.: Paraclete, 1994.

_____. *The Sacrament of the Present Moment*. Kitty Muggeridge, trans. San Francisco: Harper & Row, 1982.

_____. *Self-Abandonment to Divine Providence*. Springfield, Ill.: Templegate, 1959.

_____. *Spiritual Letters of Jean-Pierre de Caussade*. Kitty Muggeridge, trans. Wilton, Conn.: Morehouse-Barlow, 1986.

de Sales, Francis. *Athirst for God*. Michael Hollings, ed. London: Darton, Longman and Todd, 1985.

_____. *Introduction to the Devout Life*. John K. Ryan, ed. New York: Image/Doubleday, 1955.

_____. *Thy Will Be Done: Letters to Persons in the World*. Manchester, N. H.: Sophia, 1995.

Deen, Edith. *All of the Women of the Bible*. San Francisco: HarperSanFrancisco, 1955.

_____. *The Bible's Legacy for Womanhood*. Garden City, N.Y.: Doubleday, 1969.

_____. *Great Women of the Christian Faith*. Uhrichsville, Ohio: Barbour, 1959.

Devotional Classics. Richard J. Foster and James Bryan Smith, eds. San Francisco: HarperSanFrancisco, 1990.

Devotions for Morning and Evening. Mrs. Charles E. Cowman, ed. New York: Inspirational/BBS, 1999.

Dickinson, Emily. *The Poems of Emily Dickinson*. Boston: Little, Brown and Company, 1924.

Dictionary of Saints. London: Brockhampton, 1996.

Dillard, Annie. *Holy the Firm*. New York: Bantam, 1977.

_____. *Pilgrim at Tinker Creek*. New York: *Harper's* Magazine/Harper & Row, 1974.

_____. *Teaching a Stone to Talk*. New York: HarperCollins, 2000.

_____. *Tickets for a Prayer Wheel*. Columbia, Mo.: University of Missouri, 1974.

_____. *The Writing Life*. New York: Harper & Row, 1989.

Disciplines for the Inner Life. Bob Benson and Michael W. Benson, eds. Nashville: Thomas Nelson, 1989.

Dostoevsky, Fyodor. *The Brothers Karamazov*. Constance Garnett, trans. New York: Modern Library, n.d.

The Doubleday Christian Quotation Collection. Hannah Ward and Jennifer Wild, comp. New York: Doubleday, 1998.

Downey, Michael. *Trappist: Living in the Land of Desire*. New York: Paulist, 1997.

Dyson, Freeman J. *The Sun, the Genome, and the Internet*. New York: Oxford University, 1999.

Edwards, Jonathan. *The Experience That Counts!* London: Grace Publications, 1991.

_____. *On Knowing Christ*. Carlisle, Penn.: Banner of Truth Trust, 1958.

_____. *The Religious Affections*. New Haven, Conn.: Yale University, 1954.

_____. *The Works of Jonathan Edwards*. Carlisle, Penn: Banner of Truth Trust, 1974.

Eerdmans' Handbook to the History of Christianity. Tim Dowley, ed. Grand Rapids: Eerdmans, 1977.

Eldredge, John. *The Journey of Desire*. Nashville: Thomas Nelson, 2000.

Eliot, T. S. *Christianity and Culture*. New York: Harvest/Harcourt Brace Jovanovich, 1968.

_____. *The Complete Poems and Plays, 1909-1950*. New York: Harcourt, Brace and World, 1958.

Elliot, Elizabeth. *A Path Through Suffering*. Ann Arbor, Mich.: Servant, 1990.

Ellsberg, Robert. *All Saints*. New York: Crossroad, 1997.

Ellul, Jacques. *The Technological Society*. New York: Alfred A. Knopf/Vintage, 1964.

Evans, Debra. *Beauty and the Best*. Colorado Springs: Focus on the Family, 1993.

_____. *Beauty for Ashes*. Wheaton, Ill.: Crossway, 1988.

_____. *Fragrant Offerings*. Wheaton, Ill.: Crossway, 1988.

_____. *Heart & Home*. Wheaton, Ill.: Crossway, 1988.

_____. *The Christian Woman's Guide to Childbirth*. Wheaton, Ill.: Crossway, 1999.

_____. *Women of Character*. Grand Rapids: Zondervan, 1996.

_____. *Women of Courage*. Grand Rapids: Zondervan, 1999.

Evans, Jill. *Beloved & Chosen*. Norwich, Norfolk/Great Britain: Canterbury, 1993.

Fairlie, Henry. *The Seven Deadly Sins Today*. New York: Simon and Schuster, 1978.

Farmer, David Hugh. *The Oxford Dictionary of Saints*, 3rd. ed. Oxford: Oxford University, 1992.

Fastré, J. A. M. *The Acts of the Early Martyrs*. Philadelphia: Peter F. Cunningham & Son, 1885.

Fénelon, François. *Fenelon: Letters of Love and Counsel.* John McEwen, trans. New York: Harcourt, Brace and World, 1964.

Ferguson, Sinclair. *Kingdom Life in a Fallen World*. Colorado Springs: NavPress, 1986.

Fisher, M. F. K. *The Art of Eating*. Cleveland: World Publishing, 1954.

Foster, Richard J. *Celebration of Discipline*. San Francisco: HarperCollins, 1978.

_____. *Freedom of Simplicity*. San Francisco: Harper & Row, 1981.

_____. *Prayer: Finding the Heart's True Home*. San Francisco: HarperCollins, 1992.

_____. *Prayers from the Heart*. San Francisco: HarperSanFrancisco, 1994.

_____. *Richard Foster's Treasury of Christian Discipline.* New York: HarperCollins, 1988.

_____. *Seeking the Kingdom: Devotions for the Daily Journey of Faith*. San Francisco: HarperSanFrancisco, 1995.

Foxe's Book of Martyrs. New York: William L. Allison, 1890.

Francis of Assisi. *Francis and Clare: The Complete Works.* Regis J. Armstrong, trans. New York: Paulist, 1982.

Frankl, Victor E. *Man's Search for Meaning*. New York: Touchstone/Simon and Schuster, 1962.

Gariepy, Henry. *Portraits of Perseverance*. Wheaton, Ill.: Victor, 1991.

George, Bob. *Classic Christianity*. Harvest House, 1989.

Gire, Ken. *Intimate Moments with the Savior*. Grand Rapids: Zondervan, 1989.

_____. *Instructive Moments with the Savior*. Grand Rapids: Zondervan, 1992.

_____. *Windows of the Soul*. Grand Rapids: Zondervan, 1996.

Gordon, S. D. *Quiet Talks on Prayer*. Westwood, N.J.: The Christian Library, 1984.

Great Devotional Classics. Douglas V. Steere, ed. Nashville: Upper Room, 1961.

Griffin, Emilie. *Clinging: The Experience of Prayer*. New York: Harper & Row, 1984.

_____. *Wilderness Time*. San Francisco: HarperSanFrancisco, 1997.

Guinness, Os. *The Dust of Death*. Wheaton, Ill.: Crossway, 1994.

_____. *In Two Minds: The Dilemma of Doubt and How to Resolve It*. Downers Grove, Ill.: InterVarsity, 1977.

_____. *Steering Through Chaos*. Colorado Springs: NavPress, 2000.

_____. *When No One Sees*. Colorado Springs: NavPress, 2000.

Guyon, Jeanne. *Experiencing the Depths of Jesus Christ*. Auburn, Me.: Seed Sowers, 1995.

Hansen, Ron. *A Stay Against Confusion*. New York: HarperCollins, 2001.

Harris, Roberta L. *The World of the Bible*. London: Thames & Hudson, 1995.

Havergal, Frances Ridley. *Kept for the Master's Use*. New York: Grosset & Dunlap, n.d.

Hellmich, Nanci. "Innovative Fat-Fighter Jean Nidetch," *USA Today*, May 18, 1993, 1D.

Henry, Matthew. *Matthew Henry's Commentary on the Whole Bible*. Grand Rapids: Regency/Zondervan, 1960.

Herbert, George. *The Poems of George Herbert*. London: Oxford University, 1961.

His Victorious Dwelling. Nick Harrison, ed. Grand Rapids: Zondervan, 1998.

Hosier, Helen Kooiman. *100 Christian Women Who Changed the 20th Century*. Old Tappan, N.J.: Fleming H. Revell, 2000.

Houston, James. *In Pursuit of Happiness: Finding Genuine Fulfillment in Life*. Colorado Springs: NavPress, 1996.

_____. *The Heart's Desire*. Colorado Springs: NavPress, 1996.

_____. *The Transforming Friendship: A Guide to Prayer*. Oxford: Lion, 1989.

_____. *The Transforming Power of Prayer*. Colorado Springs: NavPress, 1996.

Huggett, Joyce. *The Joy of Listening to God*. Downers Grove, Ill.: InterVarsity, 1986.

_____. *Learning the Language of Prayer*. New York: Crossroad, 1986.

_____. *Listening to God*. London: Hodder and Stoughton, 1986.

Hunter, W. Bingham. *The God Who Hears*. Downers Grove, Ill.: InterVarsity, 1986.

Ignatius of Loyola. *The Spiritual Exercises of St. Ignatius*. Anthony Mottola, trans. New York: Image/Doubleday, 1964.

In Her Words: Women's Writings in the History of Christian Thought. Amy Oden, ed. Nashville: Abingdon, 1994.

Johnson, Paul. *A History of the Jews*. New York: HarperPerennial, 1987.

_____. *Birth of the Modern*. New York: HarperCollins, 1991.

_____. *The Quest for God: A Personal Pilgrimage*. New York: HarperCollins, 1996.

Joy and Strength. Mary W. Tileston, comp. New York: Barnes and Noble, 1993.

Julian of Norwich. *Showings*. Edmund Colledge and James Walsh, eds. New York: Paulist, 1978.

Keener, Craig S. *The IVP Bible Background Commentary: New Testament*. Downers Grove, Ill.: InterVarsity, 1993.

Kelly, Thomas. *A Testament of Devotion*. San Francisco: HarperSanFrancisco, 1992.

Kempis, Thomas à. *The Imitation of Christ*. William C. Creasy, trans. Macon, Ga.: Mercer University, 1989.

Kent, Carol. *Secret Longings of the Heart*. Colorado Springs: NavPress, 1990.

Kepler, Thomas S. *A Journey with the Saints*. Cleveland: World Publishing, 1951.

Keyes, Dick. *Beyond Identity: Finding Your Self in the Image and Character of God*. Ann Arbor, Mich.: Servant, 1984.

Kidd, Sue Monk. *God's Joyful Surprise: Finding Yourself Loved*. San Francisco: Harper & Row, 1987.

_____. *When the Heart Waits*. San Francisco: Harper & Row, 1990.

Kierkegaard, Soren. *A Kierkegaard Anthology*. New York: Modern Library, 1959.

_____. *Purity of Heart Is to Will One Thing*. New York: Harper/The Cloister Library, 1956.

Kilby, Clyde S. *The Christian World of C. S. Lewis*. Grand Rapids: Eerdmans, 1964.

King, Martin Luther. *Strength to Love*. New York: Collins, 1977.

Kirkpatrick, A. F. *The Book of Psalms*. Grand Rapids: Baker, 1982.

Koczak, Jan and Mark Stokoe. *Women Martyrs of the Lord*. Syosset, N.Y.: Orthodox Church in America, 1981.

Kreeft, Peter. *Back to Virtue*. San Francisco: Ignatius, 1992.

_____. *Making Sense Out of Suffering*. Ann Arbor, Mich.: Servant, 1986.

Lasch, Christopher. *The Culture of Narcissism*. New York: W. W. Norton, 1979.

Law, William. *A Serious Call to a Devout and Holy Life*. New York: Paulist, 1878.

Leclerq, John. *The Love of Learning and the Desire for God: A Study of Monastic Culture*. New York: Fordham University, 1982.

Lewis, C. S. *The Abolition of Man*. New York: Macmillan, 1955.

_____. *The Four Loves*. London: Geoffrey Bles, 1960.

_____. *God in the Dock: Essays on Theology and Ethics*. Grand Rapids: Eerdmans, 1972.

_____. *The Great Divorce*. New York: Macmillan, 1946.

_____. *Letters to Malcolm: Chiefly on Prayer*. New York: Harvest/Harcourt Brace Jovanovich, 1964.

_____. *The Lion, the Witch and the Wardrobe*. New York: Macmillan, 1950.

_____. *Mere Christianity*. New York: Macmillan, 1960.

_____. *Miracles*. New York: Macmillan, 1960.

_____. *Out of the Silent Planet*. New York: Macmillan, 1965.

_____. *Perelandra*. New York: Macmillan, 1965.

_____. *The Problem of Pain*. New York: Macmillan, 1977.

_____. *Reflections on the Psalms*. New York: Harvest/Harcourt, Brace, Jovanovich, 1958.

_____. *The Screwtape Letters*. New York: Macmillan, 1948.

_____. *Screwtape Proposes a Toast*. London: Fontana, 1965.

_____. *The Seeing Eye*. Walter Hooper, ed. New York: Ballantine, 1967.

_____. *Surprised by Joy*. New York: Harcourt, Brace and Company, 1955.

_____. *That Hideous Strength*. New York: Macmillan, 1965.

_____. *The Visionary Christian*. Chad Walsh, ed. New York: Macmillan, 1981.

Lindbergh, Anne Morrow. *Gift from the Sea*. New York: Pantheon, 1955.

Linnemann, Eta. *Jesus of the Parables.* New York: Harper & Row, 1966.

The Lion Prayer Collection. Mary Batchelor, comp. Oxford: Lion, 1996.

The Lives of the Saints. Omer Engelbert, ed. New York: Barnes and Noble, 1994.

The Living Bible. Wheaton, Ill.: Tyndale, 1971.

Llewelyn, Robert, ed. *The Joy of the Saints*. Springfield, Ill.: Templegate, 1989.

Lloyd-Jones, D. Martyn. *Alive in Christ*. Carolyn Nystrom, comp. Wheaton, Ill.: Crossway, 1997.

_____. *The Cross*. Christopher Catherwood, ed. Wheaton, Ill.: Crossway, 1986.

_____. *God's Way of Reconciliation*. Grand Rapids: Baker, 1972.

_____. *Joy Unspeakable: Power and Renewal in the Holy Spirit*. Christopher Catherwood, ed. Wheaton, Ill.: Shaw, 1984.

_____. *Romans: An Exposition of Chapter 6—The New Man*. Edinburgh: Banner of Truth Trust, 1972.

Lucado, Max. *Grace for the Moment*. Nashville: J. Countryman, 2000.

Luther, Martin. *Alone with God*. Theodore J. Kleinhans, ed. St. Louis, Mo.: Concordia, 1962.

Lyra Anglicana. George T. Rider, ed. New York: D. Appleton, 1865.

Macartney, Clarence Edward. *Great Women of the Bible*. Grand Rapids: Kregel, 1991.

Macdonald, George. *At the Back of the North Wind*. London: J. M. Dent and Sons, 1956.

_____. *Donal Grant*. Boston: D. Lothrop, 1883.

_____. *The Lost Princess: A Double Story*. London: J. M. Dent and Sons, 1967.

_____. *Sir Gibbie*. Elizabeth Yates, ed. New York: Schocken, 1979.

Macy, Howard. *Rhythms of the Inner Life*. Old Tappan, N.J.: Fleming H. Revell, 1988.

Manning, Brennan. *Abba's Child*. Colorado Springs: NavPress, 1994.

Marty, Martin. *A Cry of Absence*. San Francisco: Harper & Row, 1983.

Matheson, George. *Messages of Hope*. London: James Clarke, 1908.

_____. *Portraits of Bible Women*. Grand Rapids: Kregel, 1987.

Mathewes-Green, Frederica. *Facing East*. San Francisco: HarperSanFrancisco, 1997.

Matthews, Victor H. *Manners and Customs in Bible Times*. Peabody, Mass.: Hendrickson, 1988.

May, Gerald G. *Addiction and Grace*. Harper & Row, 1988.

May, William F. *A Catalogue of Sins: A Contemporary Examination of Christian Conscience*. New York: Holt, Rinehart and Winston, 1967.

McGinley, Phyllis. *Saint-Watching*. New York: Viking, 1969.

McGrath, Alister. *Understanding Jesus*. Grand Rapids: Zondervan, 1988.

McLaren, Alexander. *Christ in the Heart*. Funk & Wagnalls, 1905.

McIntyre, David M. *The Hidden Life of Prayer*. Denville, N.J.: Dimension, 1971.

Medwick, Cathleen. *Teresa of Avila: The Progress of a Soul*. New York: Image/Doubleday, 1999.

Menninger, Karl. *Whatever Became of Sin?* New York: Hawthorne, 1972.

Merton, Thomas. *Contemplative Prayer*. Garden City, N.J.: Image/Doubleday, 1971.

_____. *New Seeds of Contemplation*. New York: New Directions, 1961.

Michener, James. *The Source*. New York: Random House, 1965.

Miller, Calvin. *Walking with Saints*. Nashville: Thomas Nelson, 1995.

Miller, J. Keith. *Sin: Overcoming the Ultimate Deadly Addiction*. New York: Harper & Row, 1987.

_____. *The Taste of New Wine*. Waco, Tex.: Word, 1965.

Moore, K. *She for God*. London: Allison and Busby, 1978.

More, Hannah. *Practical Piety*. New York: Appleton, 1854.

_____. *Religion of the Heart*, Hal M. Helms, ed. Orleans, Mass.: Paraclete, 1993.

_____. *The Works of Hannah More, Vol. 1 and 2.* New York: Harper & Brothers, 1841.

Morgan, Tom. *Saints*. San Francisco: Chronicle, 1994.

Muggeridge, Malcolm. *Jesus: The Man Who Lives*. New York: Harper & Row, 1975.

_____. *Jesus Rediscovered*. Garden City, N.Y.: Doubleday, 1969.

Mullholland, M. Robert. *Shaped by the Word: The Power of Scripture in Spiritual Formation*. Nashville: Upper Room, 1985.

Munger, Robert Boyd. *My Heart—Christ's Home*. Downers Grove, Ill.: InterVarsity, 1992.

Murray, Andrew. *Abide in Christ*. Old Tappan, N.J.: Spire/Fleming H. Revell, n.d.

_____. *The School of Obedience*. Chicago: Moody, n.d.

_____. *Waiting on God*. Chicago: Moody, n.d.

_____. *With Christ in the School of Prayer*. Old Tappan, N.J.: Fleming H. Revell, 1975.

My Heart Sings. Joan Winmill Brown, ed. Waco, Tex.: Word, 1987.

Nee, Watchman. *The Latent Power of the Soul*. New York: Christian Fellowship, 1972.

The New Encyclopedia of Christian Quotations. Mark Water, comp. Grand Rapids: Baker, 2000.

The New English Bible. New York: Oxford University, 1961.

The NIV Study Bible. Grand Rapids: Zondervan, 1985.

Nouwen, Henri. *Bread for the Journey: A Daybook of Wisdom and Faith.* San Francisco: HarperSanFrancisco, 1997.

_____. *Making All Things New: An Invitation to the Spiritual Life.* New York: Harper & Row, 1981.

_____. *The Living Reminder: Service and Prayer in Memory of Jesus Christ*. New York: Seabury, 1977.

_____. *The Only Necessary Thing: Living a Prayerful Life*. Wendy Wilson Greer, ed. New York: Crossroad, 1999.

_____. *The Road to Daybreak*. New York: Doubleday, 1988.

_____. *The Way of the Heart*. New York: Ballantine, 1981.

_____. *With Open Hands*. Notre Dame, Ind.: Ave Maria, 1972.

Norris, Kathleen. *Amazing Grace: A Vocabulary of Faith*. New York: Riverhead, 1998.

_____. *The Cloister Walk*. New York: Riverhead, 1996.

O'Connor, Flannery. *The Habit of Being: Letters of Flannery O'Connor*. Sally Fitzgerald, ed. New York: Farrar, Straus, Giroux, 1979.

_____. *Mystery and Manners*. Robert and Sally Fitzgerald, eds. New York: Farrar, Straus, Giroux, 1969.

On Being Christian. Armand Eisen, ed. Kansas City, Mo.: Ariel/Andrews and McMeel, 1995.

One Holy Passion: Growing Deeper in Your Walk with God. Judith Couchman, comp. Colorado Springs: Waterbrook, 1998.

The One Year Book of Personal Prayer. Wheaton, Ill.: Tyndale, 1991.

The Oxford Book of Prayer. George Appleton, ed. Oxford: Oxford University, 1985.

Packer, J. I. *Knowing God*. Downers Grove, Ill.: InterVarsity, 1973.

Palms, Roger C. *The Pleasure of His Company*. Wheaton, Ill.: Tyndale, 1982.

Pascal, Blaise. *Pensées*. New York: Dutton, 1958.

Peace, Richard. *Contemplative Bible Reading: Experiencing God Through Scripture*. Colorado Springs: NavPress, 1996.

_____. *Spiritual Storytelling: Discovering and Sharing Your Spiritual Autobiography*. Colorado Springs: NavPress, 1996.

Peck, M. Scott. *The Road Less Traveled*. New York: Simon and Schuster, 1978.

Peterson, Eugene H. *A Long Obedience in the Same Direction*. Downers Grove, Ill.: InterVarsity, 1980.

_____. *Answering God: The Psalms As Tools for Prayer*. San Francisco: HarperSanFrancisco, 1989.

_____. *Earth and Altar.* Downers Grove, Ill.: InterVarsity, 1985.

_____. *The Message*. Colorado Springs: NavPress, 1994.

_____. *Praying with Jesus.* San Francisco: HarperCollins, 1993.

_____. *Run with the Horses*. Downers Grove, Ill.: InterVarsity, 1983.

_____. *Traveling Light*. Colorado Springs: Helmers & Howard, 1988.

Petrie, Ann and Jeanette. *Mother Teresa*. USA: Petrie Productions/Vision Video, 1986.

Phillips, J. B. *The Church Under the Cross.* New York: Macmillan, 1956.

_____. *The New Testament in Modern English*. New York: Macmillan, 1960.

____. *Ring of Truth*. London: Hodder and Stoughton, 1967.

Pilgrim Souls: A Collection of Spiritual Autobiographies. Amy Mandelker and Elizabeth Powers, eds. New York: Simon and Schuster, 1999.

Piper, John. *Desiring God*. Portland, Ore.: Multnomah, 1986.

Potok, Chaim. *Wanderings*. New York: Fawcett Crest/Ballantine, 1978.

Prayers: Ancient and Modern. Mary Wilder Tileston, comp. New York: Grosset & Dunlap, 1897.

Ray, David. *The Art of Christian Meditation*. Wheaton, Ill.: Tyndale, 1977.

Richards, Lawrence O. *The Bible Reader's Companion*. Wheaton, Ill.: Victor, 1991.

Ringma, Charles. *Seize the Day with Dietrich Bonhoeffer*. Colorado Springs: Piñon, 2000.

Rossetti, Christina. *Goblin Market and Other Poems*. London: Macmillan, 1862.

Ryken, Leland. *Culture in Christian Perspective*. Portland, Ore.: Multnomah, 1986.

Sanders, J. Oswald. *Enjoying Intimacy with God*. Chicago: Moody, 1980.

Sayers, Dorothy. *A Matter of Eternity*. Grand Rapids: Eerdmans, 1973.

_____. *Are Women Human?* Grand Rapids: Eerdmans, 1971.

_____. *Christian Letters to a Post-Christian World*. Grand Rapids: Eerdmans, 1969.

_____. *Creed or Chaos?* London: Hodder and Stoughton, 1949.

_____. *The Man Born to Be King*. Grand Rapids: Eerdmans, n.d.

_____. *The Mind of the Maker*. Westport, Conn.: Greenwood, 1970.

_____. *The Other Six Deadly Sins*. London: Methuen, 1943.

_____. *The Whimsical Christian*. William Griffin, ed. New York: Macmillan, 1978.

Schaef, Ann Wilson. *When Society Becomes an Addict*. San Francisco: Harper & Row, 1987.

Schaeffer, Edith. *A Way of Seeing*. Old Tappan, N.J.: Fleming H. Revell, 1977.

_____. *Affliction*. Old Tappan, N.J.: Fleming H. Revell, 1978.

_____. *The Art of Life*. Louis G. Parkhurst, ed. Wheaton, Ill.: Crossway, 1987.

_____. *Christianity Is Jewish*. Wheaton, Ill.: Tyndale, 1975.

_____. *Common Sense Christian Living*. Nashville: Thomas Nelson, 1983.

_____. *L'Abri*. Wheaton, Ill.: Tyndale, 1970.

_____. *Lifelines: The Ten Commandments for Today*. New York: Ballantine, 1982.

_____. *What Is a Family?* Old Tappan, N.J.: Fleming H. Revell, 1975.

Schaeffer, Francis. *The Francis Schaeffer Trilogy*. Wheaton, Ill.: Crossway, 1990.

_____. *True Spirituality*. Wheaton, Ill.: Tyndale, 1971.

Schlink, M. Basilea. *Repentance: The Joy-filled Life*. Grand Rapids: Zondervan, 1968.

Schlossberg, Herbert. *Idols for Destruction*. Wheaton, Ill.: Crossway, 1990.

Seid, Roberta Pollack. *Never Too Thin: Why Women Are at War with Their Bodies*. New York: Prentice Hall, 1989.

Shelley, Bruce. *All the Saints Adore Thee*. Grand Rapids: Baker, 1988.

Smith, Hannah Whitall. *The Christian's Secret of a Happy Life*. Westwood, N.J.: Spire/Fleming H. Revell, 1970.

Snyder, Howard. *The Community of the King*. Downers Grove, Ill.: InterVarsity, 1977.

Sommerfeldt, John R. *The Spiritual Teachings of Bernard of Clairvaux*. Kalamazoo, Mich.: Cistercian, 1991.

Spiritual Awakenings: Classic Writings of the 18th Century to Inspire the 20th Century Reader. Sherwood Eliot Wirt, ed. Wheaton, Ill.: Crossway, 1986.

Spiritual Classics. Richard J. Foster and Emilie Griffin, eds. San Francisco: HarperSanFrancisco, 2000.

Spiritual Witness: Classic Christian Writings of the Twentieth Century. Sherwood Eliot Wirt, ed. Wheaton, Ill.: Crossway, 1991.

Sproul, R. C. *The Holiness of God*. Wheaton, Ill.: Tyndale, 1985.

_____. *Pleasing God*. Wheaton, Ill.: Tyndale, 1988.

_____. *The Soul's Quest for God*. Wheaton, Ill.: Tyndale, 1992.

Spurgeon, Charles Haddon. *All of Grace*. Springdale, Penn.: Whitaker, 1983.

_____. *Morning and Evening*. Grand Rapids: Zondervan, 1960.

_____. *Psalms*. David Otis Fuller, ed. Grand Rapids: Kregel, 1968.

_____. *The Treasury of David*, Vol. 1-5. London: Passmore and Alabaster, 1871.

Stafford, Tim. *Knowing the Face of God: The Search for a Personal Relationship with God*. Grand Rapids: Zondervan, 1986.

Stott, John R. W. *Baptism and Fullness: The Work of the Holy Spirit Today*. Downers Grove, Ill.: InterVarsity, 1976.

_____. *Basic Christianity*. Grand Rapids: Eerdmans, 1965.

_____. *Basic Introduction to the New Testament*. Downers Grove, Ill.: InterVarsity, 1964.

_____. *Christian Counter-Culture: The Message of the Sermon on the Mount*. Downers Grove, Ill.: InterVarsity, 1978.

_____. *The Cross of Christ*. Downers Grove, Ill.: InterVarsity, 1986.

_____. *Romans: God's Good News for the World*. Downers Grove, Ill.: InterVarsity, 1995.

_____. *Understanding the Bible*. London: Scripture Union, 1972.

Streams in the Desert. Mrs. Charles E. Cowman, comp. Grand Rapids: Zondervan, 1925.

Tada, Joni Eareckson. *A Quiet Place in a Crazy World*. Portland, Ore.: Multnomah, 1993.

_____. *Heaven: Your Real Home*. Grand Rapids: Zondervan, 1995.

_____. *When God Weeps: Why Our Sufferings Matter to the Almighty*. Grand Rapids: Zondervan, 1997.

Talbot, John Michael. *The Lessons of St. Francis: How to Bring Simplicity and Spirituality into Your Daily Life*. New York: Dutton, 1997.

Taylor, Jeremy. *The Rules and Exercises of Holy Dying*. Cleveland: World Publishing, 1956.

_____. *The Rules and Exercise of Holy Living*. Cleveland: World Publishing, 1956.

ten Boom, Corrie. *Each New Day*. Minneapolis: World Wide, 1977.

_____. *The Hiding Place*. Uhrichsville, Ohio: Barbour, 1971.

_____. *Not I, But Christ*. Nashville: Thomas Nelson, 1983.

Teresa of Avila. *A Life of Prayer*. James L. Houston, ed. Portland, Ore.: Multnomah, 1983.

_____. *Daily Readings with Teresa of Avila*. Sister Mary ODC, ed. Springfield, Ill.: Templegate, 1985.

_____. *The Collected Works of St. Teresa of Avila*. Kieran Kavanaugh and Otilio Rodriguez, trans. Washington, D.C.: ICS Publications, 1976.

_____. *Interior Castle*. E. Allison Peers, ed. New York: Image/Doubleday, 1961.

_____. *The Life of Saint Teresa of Avila by Herself.* J. M. Cohen, trans. New York: Penguin, 1957.

_____. *Majestic Is Your Name*. David Hazard, comp. Minneapolis: Bethany, 1993.

_____. *The Way of Perfection*. E. Allison Peers, ed. New York: Image/Doubleday, 1964.

Teresa of Calcutta. *A Simple Path*. Lucinda Vardey, comp. New York: Ballantine, 1995.

_____. *Blessed Are You*. Eileen Egan and Kathleen Egan, eds. Ann Arbor, Mich.: Servant, 1992.

_____. *Love Is Always a Fruit in Season*. Dorothy S. Hunt, ed. San Francisco: Ignatius, 1987.

Thérèse of Lisieux. *By Love Alone*. Michael Hollings, ed. London: Darton, Longman and Todd, 1986.

_____. *Poems*. Alan Bancroft, trans. New York: Fount/HarperCollins, 1996.

Thurman, Howard. *Deep Is the Hunger*. New York: Harper & Brothers, 1951.

Timmermans, Felix. *The Perfect Joy of St. Francis*. New York: Image/Doubleday, 1955.

Today's Parallel Bible: New International Version/New American Standard Bible/King James Version/New Living Translation. Grand Rapids: Zondervan, 2000.

Toon, Peter. *Spiritual Companions: An Introduction to the Christian Classics*. Grand Rapids: Baker, 1990.

Topping, Eva Catafygiotu. *Saints and Sisterhood: The Lives of Forty-Eight Holy Women*. Minneapolis: Light and Life, 1990.

Torrey, R. A. *How to Pray*. Old Tappan, N.J.: Fleming H. Revell, 1900.

Tozer, A. W. *Best of A. W. Tozer*. Warren Weirsbe, ed. Camp Hill, Penn.: Christian Publications, 1979.

_____. *The Divine Conquest*. Wheaton, Ill.: Tyndale, 1995.

_____. *Gems from Tozer*. Camp Hill, Penn.: Christian Publications, 1971.

_____. *High Mountains, Deep Valleys*. Sutherland, Australia: Albatross, 1991.

_____. *Keys to the Deeper Life*. Grand Rapids: Zondervan, 1984.

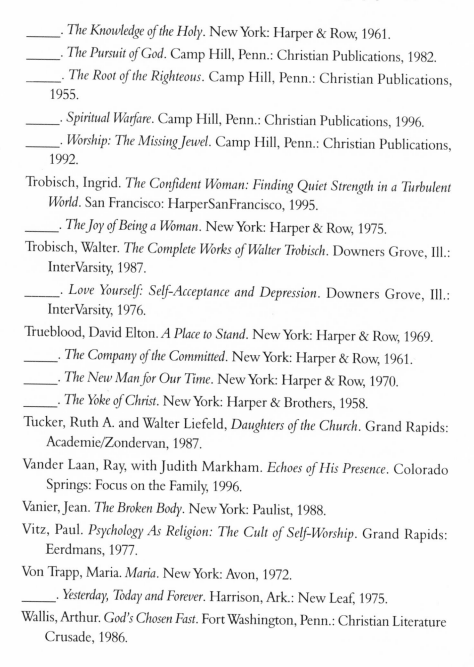

_____. *The Knowledge of the Holy*. New York: Harper & Row, 1961.

_____. *The Pursuit of God*. Camp Hill, Penn.: Christian Publications, 1982.

_____. *The Root of the Righteous*. Camp Hill, Penn.: Christian Publications, 1955.

_____. *Spiritual Warfare*. Camp Hill, Penn.: Christian Publications, 1996.

_____. *Worship: The Missing Jewel*. Camp Hill, Penn.: Christian Publications, 1992.

Trobisch, Ingrid. *The Confident Woman: Finding Quiet Strength in a Turbulent World*. San Francisco: HarperSanFrancisco, 1995.

_____. *The Joy of Being a Woman*. New York: Harper & Row, 1975.

Trobisch, Walter. *The Complete Works of Walter Trobisch*. Downers Grove, Ill.: InterVarsity, 1987.

_____. *Love Yourself: Self-Acceptance and Depression*. Downers Grove, Ill.: InterVarsity, 1976.

Trueblood, David Elton. *A Place to Stand*. New York: Harper & Row, 1969.

_____. *The Company of the Committed*. New York: Harper & Row, 1961.

_____. *The New Man for Our Time*. New York: Harper & Row, 1970.

_____. *The Yoke of Christ*. New York: Harper & Brothers, 1958.

Tucker, Ruth A. and Walter Liefeld, *Daughters of the Church*. Grand Rapids: Academie/Zondervan, 1987.

Vander Laan, Ray, with Judith Markham. *Echoes of His Presence*. Colorado Springs: Focus on the Family, 1996.

Vanier, Jean. *The Broken Body*. New York: Paulist, 1988.

Vitz, Paul. *Psychology As Religion: The Cult of Self-Worship*. Grand Rapids: Eerdmans, 1977.

Von Trapp, Maria. *Maria*. New York: Avon, 1972.

_____. *Yesterday, Today and Forever*. Harrison, Ark.: New Leaf, 1975.

Wallis, Arthur. *God's Chosen Fast*. Fort Washington, Penn.: Christian Literature Crusade, 1986.

Ward, Benedicta. *Daily Readings with the Desert Fathers*. Springfield, Ill.: Templegate, 1990.

Ware, Kallistos. *The Orthodox Way*. Crestwood, N.Y.: St. Vladimir's Seminary, 1995.

Watson, David C. K. *In Search of God*. London: Falcon, 1974.

Weatherhead, Leslie D. *Prescription for Anxiety*. New York: Abingdon, 1956.

_____. *Salute to a Sufferer*. New York: Abingdon, 1962.

_____. *Why Do Men Suffer?* New York: Abingdon, 1936.

Weirsbe, Warren. *A Time to Be Renewed*. Wheaton, Ill.: Victor, 1986.

Wesley, John. *The Christian's Pattern*. New York: Abingdon, n.d.

_____. *The Gift of Love*. Arthur Skevington Wood, ed. London: Darton, Longman and Todd, 1987.

_____. *The New Birth*. Thomas C. Oden, ed. New York: Harper & Row, 1984.

White, John. *Changing on the Inside*. Ann Arbor, Mich.: Vine, 1991.

_____. *The Cost of Commitment*. Downers Grove, Ill.: InterVarsity, 1976.

_____. *Daring to Draw Near*. Downers Grove, Ill.: InterVarsity, 1977.

_____. *The Fight*. Downers Grove, Ill.: InterVarsity, 1976.

_____. *Flirting with the World: A Challenge to Loyalty*. Wheaton, Ill.: Shaw, 1982.

_____. *The Golden Cow*. Downers Grove, Ill.: InterVarsity, 1979.

White, Kristin E. *A Guide to the Saints*. New York: Ballantine, 1991.

Whitney, Donald S. *Spiritual Disciplines for the Christian Life*. Colorado Springs: NavPress, 1991.

Wiesel, Elie. *Sages and Dreamers*. New York: Summit/Simon and Schuster, 1991.

Wilberforce, William. *Real Christianity*. Portland, Ore.: Multnomah, 1982.

Willard, Dallas. *In Search of Guidance: Developing a Conversational Relationship with God*. San Francisco: HarperSanFrancisco/Zondervan, 1993.

_____. *The Divine Conspiracy: Rediscovering Our Hidden Life in God*. San Francisco: HarperSanFrancisco, 1998.

_____. *The Spirit of the Disciplines: Understanding How God Changes Lives*. San Francisco: Harper & Row, 1988.

Wilson, Angus, W. H. Auden, et al. *The Seven Deadly Sins*. New York: William Morrow, 1992.

Wilson, Marvin R. *Our Father Abraham: The Jewish Roots of the Christian Faith*. Grand Rapids: Eerdmans, 1989.

Wilson-Kastner, Patricia. *A Lost Tradition: Women Writers of the Early Church*. Lanham, New York and London: University Press of America, 1981.

Wisdom of the Saints. Jill Haak Adels, ed. New York: Oxford University, 1987.

Women in Scripture. Carol Meyers, ed. Boston: Houghton Mifflin, 2000.

The World's Great Religious Poetry. Carolyn Miles Hill, ed. New York: Macmillan, 1925.

Wright, Elliott. *Holy Company: Christian Heroes and Heroines*. New York: Macmillan, 1980.

Yancey, Philip. *Disappointment with God*. Grand Rapids: Zondervan, 1988.

_____. *Finding God in Unexpected Places*. Nashville: Moorings, 1995.

_____. *The Jesus I Never Knew*. Grand Rapids: Zondervan, 1995.

_____. *Reaching for the Invisible God: What Can We Expect to Find?* Grand Rapids: Zondervan, 2000.

_____. *What's So Amazing About Grace?* Grand Rapids: Zondervan, 1997.

_____. *Where Is God When It Hurts?* Grand Rapids: Zondervan, 1977.

Young, Brad H. *Jesus and His Jewish Parables*. Mahwah, N.J.: Paulist, 1989.

_____. *Jesus the Jewish Theologian*. Peabody, Mass.: Hendrickson, 1995.

Zefferelli, Franco. *Brother Sun, Sister Moon*. UK/Italy: Paramount/Vic Films/Euro International, 1972.

Zondervan Exhaustive Concordance. Edward W. Goodrick, John R. Kohlenberger III, and James A. Swanson, eds. Grand Rapids: Zondervan, 1999.

Scripture List

Chapter 3

Chapter 4

Chapter 5

Chapter 6

Workbook

None Like You:
A Personal Workbook

Those who live in the shelter of the Most High will find rest in the shadow of the Almighty. This I declare of the Lord: He alone is my refuge, my place of safety; he is my God, and I am trusting him. (Ps. 91:1-2 NLT)

To be silent does not mean to be inactive; rather it means to breathe in the will of God, to listen attentively and be ready to obey.

DIETRICH BONHOEFFER

He therefore keeps the secret key Himself
To open all the chambers, and to bless
With perfect sympathy, and holy peace,
Each solitary soul which comes to Him.

—ANONYMOUS

I have stilled and quieted my soul. (Ps. 131:2)

In my singing and my silence,
Lord, be glorified.
In my decisions and my dreams,
Lord, be glorified.
In my loves and my hates,
Lord, be glorified.
In my accomplishments and my mistakes,
Lord, be glorified.
In my contentment and my disappointment,
Lord, be glorified.
In my celebrating and my sorrow,
Lord, be glorified.
In my knowledge and my doubt,
Lord, be glorified.
In my courage and my fear,
Lord, be glorified.
In my satisfaction and my hunger,
Lord, be glorified.

Lord,
in my body,
in my mind,
in my heart,
and in my spirit—
be glorified!
In Jesus' name, I pray.
Amen.

Feed on God's Word

> *One thing I ask of the LORD, this is what I seek: that I may dwell in the house of the LORD all the days of my life, to gaze upon the beauty of the LORD and to seek him in his temple. For in the day of trouble he will keep me safe in his dwelling; he will hide me in the shelter of his tabernacle and set me high upon a rock. (Ps. 27:4-5)*

Taste . . .

Recognize and honor the Lord's presence as you slowly read the passage. After reading the verse two or three times, try repeating the words with your eyes closed. Direct your mind and heart toward Jesus as your thoughts dwell on His Word in silence.

What worry, concern, or burden do you need to surrender to Christ right now so that you may more mindfully enter His presence?

Chew . . .

Listen in faith to the Lord speaking to you in His Word. Reflect upon the words in this passage with a willingness to obey God's direction, inviting Him to shape your soul's appetites and attitudes according to His design for your life.

What words, pictures, phrases, thoughts, impressions, and feelings stay with you as you meditate on this verse?

Savor . . .

Enjoy God's provision for your heart, soul, body, and mind. Welcome His Word with prayers of thanksgiving, confession, blessing, acknowledgment, adoration, praise, petition, and appreciation.

Where does the Holy Spirit seem to be pointing your attention as you reread and ponder this passage?

Swallow . . .

Receive the nourishing strength imparted to you through God's Word. Seek His wisdom, help, and understanding as His truth revives your soul.

What do you sense the Lord wants you to know, feel, or do in response to reading this passage?

DIGEST . . .

Remain with Jesus for a while longer in stillness. Rest in His presence, waiting upon His Word. Gently draw your attention back to the main passage whenever your mind wanders.

What is it you most want to say to Jesus at this moment?

So may the LORD be a tower of strength for the oppressed, a tower of strength in time of need, that those who acknowledge thy name may trust in thee; for thou, LORD, dost not forsake those who seek thee. (Ps. 9:9-10 NEB)

O Saviour, how unspeakable is Thy love! "Such knowledge is too wonderful for me: it is high, I cannot attain to it." I can only yield myself to Thy love with the prayer that, day by day, Thou wouldst unfold to me somewhat of its precious mysteries, and so encourage and strengthen Thy loving disciple to do what his heart longs to do indeed—ever, only, wholly to abide in Thee.

ANDREW MURRAY

Feed on God's Word

How precious is your unfailing love, O God! All humanity finds shelter in the shadow of your wings. You feed them from the abundance of your own house, letting them drink from your rivers of delight. For you are the fountain of life, the light by which we see. (Ps. 36:7-9 NLT)

Taste . . .

Recognize and honor the Lord's presence as you slowly read the passage. After reading the verse two or three times, try repeating the words with your eyes closed. Direct your mind and heart toward Jesus as your thoughts dwell on His Word in silence.

What worry, concern, or burden do you need to surrender to Christ right now so that you may more mindfully enter His presence?

Chew . . .

Listen in faith to the Lord speaking to you in His Word. Reflect upon the words in this passage with a willingness to obey God's direction, inviting Him to shape your soul's appetites and attitudes according to His design for your life.

What words, pictures, phrases, thoughts, impressions, and feelings stay with you as you meditate on this verse?

SAVOR . . .

Enjoy God's provision for your heart, soul, body, and mind. Welcome His Word with prayers of thanksgiving, confession, blessing, acknowledgment, adoration, praise, petition, and appreciation.

Where does the Holy Spirit seem to be pointing your attention as you reread and ponder this passage?

SWALLOW . . .

Receive the nourishing strength imparted to you through God's Word. Seek His wisdom, help, and understanding as His truth revives your soul.

What do you sense the Lord wants you to know, feel, or do in response to reading this passage?

DIGEST . . .

Remain with Jesus for a while longer in stillness. Rest in His presence, waiting upon His Word. Gently draw your attention back to the main passage whenever your mind wanders.

What is it you most want to say to Jesus at this moment?

Surely your goodness and unfailing love will pursue me all the days of my life, and I will live in the house of the LORD forever. (Ps. 23:6 NLT)

Satisfied with God, rejoicing in Christ, full of the Holy Spirit, the weakest believer may well be wondered at by men of the earth who feel an incessant craving for they know not what.

GEORGE V. WIGRAM

Feed on God's Word

O LORD, my heart is not proud, nor are my eyes haughty; I do not busy myself with great matters or things too marvelous for me. No, I submit myself, I account myself lowly, as a weaned child clinging to its mother. (Ps. 131:1-2 NEB)

TASTE . . .

Recognize and honor the Lord's presence as you slowly read the passage. After reading the verse two or three times, try repeating the words with your eyes closed. Direct your mind and heart toward Jesus as your thoughts dwell on His Word in silence.

What worry, concern, or burden do you need to surrender to Christ right now, so that you may more mindfully enter His presence?

CHEW . . .

Listen in faith to the Lord speaking to you in His Word. Reflect upon the words in this passage with a willingness to obey God's direction, inviting Him to shape your soul's appetites and attitudes according to His design for your life.

What words, pictures, phrases, thoughts, impressions, and feelings stay with you as you meditate on this verse?

Savor . . .

Enjoy God's provision for your heart, soul, body, and mind. Welcome His Word with prayers of thanksgiving, confession, blessing, acknowledgment, adoration, praise, petition, and appreciation.

Where does the Holy Spirit seem to be pointing your attention as you reread and ponder this passage?

Swallow . . .

Receive the nourishing strength imparted to you through God's Word. Seek His wisdom, help, and understanding as His truth revives your soul.

What do you sense the Lord wants you to know, feel, or do in response to reading this passage?

DIGEST . . .

Remain with Jesus for a while longer in stillness. Rest in His presence, waiting upon His Word. Gently draw your attention back to the main passage whenever your mind wanders.

What is it you most want to say to Jesus at this moment?

Let your face shine on your servant; save me in your unfailing love. (Ps. 31:16)

Father in heaven, when the thought of You wakes in our hearts, let it not awaken like a frightened bird flying about in dismay, but like a child waking from its sleep with a heavenly smile.

SOREN KIERKEGAARD

Feed on God's Word

Find rest, O my soul, in God alone; my hope comes from him. He alone is my rock and my salvation; he is my fortress, I will not be shaken. My salvation and my honor depend on God; he is my mighty rock, my refuge. Trust in him at all times, O people; pour out your hearts to him, for God is our refuge. (Ps. 62:5-8)

Taste . . .

Recognize and honor the Lord's presence as you slowly read the passage. After reading the verse two or three times, try repeating the words with your eyes closed. Direct your mind and heart toward Jesus as your thoughts dwell on His Word in silence.

What worry, concern, or burden do you need to surrender to Christ right now, so that you may more mindfully enter His presence?

Chew . . .

Listen in faith to the Lord speaking to you in His Word. Reflect upon the words in this passage with a willingness to obey God's direction, inviting Him to shape your soul's appetites and attitudes according to His design for your life.

What words, pictures, phrases, thoughts, impressions, and feelings stay with you as you meditate on this verse?

SAVOR . . .

Enjoy God's provision for your heart, soul, body, and mind. Welcome His Word with prayers of thanksgiving, confession, blessing, acknowledgment, adoration, praise, petition, and appreciation.

Where does the Holy Spirit seem to be pointing your attention as you reread and ponder this passage?

Swallow . . .

Receive the nourishing strength imparted to you through God's Word. Seek His wisdom, help, and understanding as His truth revives your soul.

What do you sense the Lord wants you to know, feel, or do in response to reading this passage?

Digest . . .

Remain with Jesus for a while longer in stillness. Rest in His presence, waiting upon His Word. Gently draw your attention back to the main passage whenever your mind wanders.

What is it you most want to say to Jesus at this moment?

Because you are my help, I sing in the shadow of your wings. My soul clings to you; your right hand upholds me. (Ps. 63:7–8)

As far as you can, remain calm and even at peace in holy joy, in order so to experience all the well-being which fills a contented and joyful heart.

JEAN-PIERRE DE CAUSSADE

Feed on God's Word

> *Trust in the LORD and do good; so shalt thou dwell in the land, and verily thou shalt be fed. Delight thyself also in the LORD; and he shall give thee the desires of thine heart. Commit thy way unto the LORD; trust also in him, and he shall bring it to pass. Rest in the LORD, and wait patiently for him. (Ps. 37:3-5, 7a KJV)*

TASTE . . .

Recognize and honor the Lord's presence as you slowly read the passage. After reading the verse two or three times, try repeating the words with your eyes closed. Direct your mind and heart toward Jesus as your thoughts dwell on His Word in silence.

What worry, concern, or burden do you need to surrender to Christ right now, so that you may more mindfully enter His presence?

CHEW . . .

Listen in faith to the Lord speaking to you in His Word. Reflect upon the words in this passage with a willingness to obey God's direction, inviting Him to shape your soul's appetites and attitudes according to His design for your life.

What words, pictures, phrases, thoughts, impressions, and feelings stay with you as you meditate on this verse?

Savor . . .

Enjoy God's provision for your heart, soul, body, and mind. Welcome His Word with prayers of thanksgiving, confession, blessing, acknowledgment, adoration, praise, petition, and appreciation.

Where does the Holy Spirit seem to be pointing your attention as you reread and ponder this passage?

Swallow . . .

Receive the nourishing strength imparted to you through God's Word. Seek His wisdom, help, and understanding as His truth revives your soul.

What do you sense the Lord wants you to know, feel, or do in response to reading this passage?

DIGEST . . .

Remain with Jesus for a while longer in stillness. Rest in His presence, waiting upon His Word. Gently draw your attention back to the main passage whenever your mind wanders.

What is it you most want to say to Jesus at this moment?

Truly, my heart waits silently for God; my deliverance comes from him. (Ps. 40:1 NEB*)*

If God had not said, Blessed are those that hunger, I know not what would keep [us] from sinking in despair; many times all I can do is to find and complain that I want Him, and wish to recover Him; now this is my stay, that He in mercy esteems us not only having, but by desiring also; and, after a sort, accounts us to have that which we want and desire to have.

JOSEPH HALL

Feed on God's Word

Create a pure heart in me, O God, and give me a new and steadfast spirit; do not drive me from thy presence or take thy Holy Spirit from me; revive in me the joy of thy deliverance and grant me a willing spirit to uphold me. (Ps. 51:10-12 NEB)

Taste . . .

Recognize and honor the Lord's presence as you slowly read the passage. After reading the verse two or three times, try repeating the words with your eyes closed. Direct your mind and heart toward Jesus as your thoughts dwell on His Word in silence.

What worry, concern, or burden do you need to surrender to Christ right now, so that you may more mindfully enter His presence?

Chew . . .

Listen in faith to the Lord speaking to you in His Word. Reflect upon the words in this passage with a willingness to obey God's direction, inviting Him to shape your soul's appetites and attitudes according to His design for your life.

What words, pictures, phrases, thoughts, impressions, and feelings stay with you as you meditate on this verse?

Savor . . .

Enjoy God's provision for your heart, soul, body, and mind. Welcome His Word with prayers of thanksgiving, confession, blessing, acknowledgment, adoration, praise, petition, and appreciation.

Where does the Holy Spirit seem to be pointing your attention as you reread and ponder this passage?

Swallow . . .

Receive the nourishing strength imparted to you through God's Word. Seek His wisdom, help, and understanding as His truth revives your soul.

What do you sense the Lord wants you to know, feel, or do in response to reading this passage?

Digest . . .

Remain with Jesus for a while longer in stillness. Rest in His presence, waiting upon His Word. Gently draw your attention back to the main passage whenever your mind wanders.

What is it you most want to say to Jesus at this moment?

I will praise you, O Lord my God, with all my heart; I will glorify your name forever. For great is your love toward me; you have delivered me from the depths of the grave. (Ps. 86:12-13)

To repent is to alter one's way of looking at life; it is to take God's point of view instead of one's own.

ANONYMOUS

Feed on God's Word

> *Teach me, O LORD, to follow your decrees; then I will keep them to the end. Give me understanding, and I will keep your law and obey it with all my heart. Direct me in the path of your commands, for there I find delight. Turn my heart toward your statutes and not toward selfish gain. Turn my eyes away from worthless things; preserve my life according to your word. (Psalm 119:33-37)*

TASTE . . .

Recognize and honor the Lord's presence as you slowly read the passage. After reading the verse two or three times, try repeating the words with your eyes closed. Direct your mind and heart toward Jesus as your thoughts dwell on His Word in silence.

What worry, concern, or burden do you need to surrender to Christ right now, so that you may more mindfully enter His presence?

CHEW . . .

Listen in faith to the Lord speaking to you in His Word. Reflect upon the words in this passage with a willingness to obey God's direction, inviting Him to shape your soul's appetites and attitudes according to His design for your life.

What words, pictures, phrases, thoughts, impressions, and feelings stay with you as you meditate on this verse?

SAVOR . . .

Enjoy God's provision for your heart, soul, body, and mind. Welcome His Word with prayers of thanksgiving, confession, blessing, acknowledgment, adoration, praise, petition, and appreciation.

Where does the Holy Spirit seem to be pointing your attention as you reread and ponder this passage?

SWALLOW . . .

Receive the nourishing strength imparted to you through God's Word. Seek His wisdom, help, and understanding as His truth revives your soul.

What do you sense the Lord wants you to know, feel, or do in response to reading this passage?

DIGEST . . .

Remain with Jesus for a while longer in stillness. Rest in His presence, waiting upon His Word. Gently draw your attention back to the main passage whenever your mind wanders.

What is it you most want to say to Jesus at this moment?

Teach me your way, O LORD, and I will walk in your truth; give me an undivided heart, that I may fear your name. (Ps. 86:11)

There is no leveler like Christianity, but it levels by lifting all who receive it to the lofty table-land of a true character and of undying hope both for this world and the next.

JONATHAN EDWARDS

Feed on God's Word

Give the LORD thanks and invoke him by name, make his deeds known in the world around. Pay him honour with song and psalm and think upon all his wonders. Exult in his hallowed name; let those who seek the LORD be joyful in heart. Turn to the LORD, your strength, seek his presence always. (Ps. 105:1-4 NEB)

Taste . . .

Recognize and honor the Lord's presence as you slowly read the passage. After reading the verse two or three times, try repeating the words with your eyes closed. Direct your mind and heart toward Jesus as your thoughts dwell on His Word in silence.

What worry, concern, or burden do you need to surrender to Christ right now, so that you may more mindfully enter His presence?

Chew . . .

Listen in faith to the Lord speaking to you in His Word. Reflect upon the words in this passage with a willingness to obey God's direction, inviting Him to shape your soul's appetites and attitudes according to His design for your life.

What words, pictures, phrases, thoughts, impressions, and feelings stay with you as you meditate on this verse?

Savor . . .

Enjoy God's provision for your heart, soul, body, and mind. Welcome His Word with prayers of thanksgiving, confession, blessing, acknowledgment, adoration, praise, petition, and appreciation.

Where does the Holy Spirit seem to be pointing your attention as you reread and ponder this passage?

Swallow . . .

Receive the nourishing strength imparted to you through God's Word. Seek His wisdom, help, and understanding as His truth revives your soul.

What do you sense the Lord wants you to know, feel, or do in response to reading this passage?

Digest . . .

Remain with Jesus for a while longer in stillness. Rest in His presence, waiting upon His Word. Gently draw your attention back to the main passage whenever your mind wanders.

What is it you most want to say to Jesus at this moment?

Hear my voice when I call, O LORD; be merciful to me and answer me. My heart says of you, "Seek his face!" Your face, LORD, I will seek. Do not hide your face from me. (Ps. 27:7-8)

The true way to be humble is not to stoop until you are smaller than yourself, but to stand at your real height against some higher nature that will show you what the real smallness of your greatness is.

PHILLIPS BROOKS

Feed on God's Word

As for God, his way is perfect. All the LORD's promises prove true. He is a shield for all who look to him for protection. For who is God except the LORD? Who but our God is a solid rock? God arms me with strength; he has made my way safe. He makes me as surefooted as a deer, leading me safely along the mountain heights. He prepares me for battle; he strengthens me to draw a bow of bronze. You have given me the shield of your salvation. Your right hand supports me; your gentleness has made me great. You have made a wide path for my feet to keep them from slipping. (Ps. 18:30-36 NLT)

Taste . . .

Recognize and honor the Lord's presence as you slowly read the passage. After reading the verse two or three times, try repeating the words with your eyes closed. Direct your mind and heart toward Jesus as your thoughts dwell on His Word in silence.

What worry, concern, or burden do you need to surrender to Christ right now, so that you may more mindfully enter His presence?

Chew . . .

Listen in faith to the Lord speaking to you in His Word. Reflect upon the words in this passage with a willingness to obey God's direction, inviting Him to shape your soul's appetites and attitudes according to His design for your life.

What words, pictures, phrases, thoughts, impressions, and feelings stay with you as you meditate on this verse?

SAVOR . . .

Enjoy God's provision for your heart, soul, body, and mind. Welcome His Word with prayers of thanksgiving, confession, blessing, acknowledgment, adoration, praise, petition, and appreciation.

Where does the Holy Spirit seem to be pointing your attention as you reread and ponder this passage?

SWALLOW . . .

Receive the nourishing strength imparted to you through God's Word. Seek His wisdom, help, and understanding as His truth revives your soul.

What do you sense the Lord wants you to know, feel, or do in response to reading this passage?

DIGEST . . .

Remain with Jesus for a while longer in stillness. Rest in His presence, waiting upon His Word. Gently draw your attention back to the main passage whenever your mind wanders.

What is it you most want to say to Jesus at this moment?

Those who trust in the LORD are as secure as Mount Zion; they will not be defeated but will endure forever. Just as the mountains surround and protect Jerusalem, so the LORD surrounds and protects his people, both now and forever. (Ps. 125:1-2 NLT)

He who begins, finishes. He who leads us on, follows behind to deal in love with our poor attempts. He gathers up the things we have dropped—our fallen resolutions, our mistakes. He makes His blessed pardon to flow over our sins till they are utterly washed away. And He turns to fight the enemy, who would pursue after us, to destroy us from behind. He is first, and He is last!

AMY CARMICHAEL

Feed on God's Word

I lift up my eyes to the hills—where does my help come from? My help comes from the LORD, the Maker of heaven and earth. (Ps. 121:1-2)

Taste . . .

Recognize and honor the Lord's presence as you slowly read the passage. After reading the verse two or three times, try repeating the words with your eyes closed. Direct your mind and heart toward Jesus as your thoughts dwell on His Word in silence.

What worry, concern, or burden do you need to surrender to Christ right now, so that you may more mindfully enter His presence?

Chew . . .

Listen in faith to the Lord speaking to you in His Word. Reflect upon the words in this passage with a willingness to obey God's direction, inviting Him to shape your soul's appetites and attitudes according to His design for your life.

What words, pictures, phrases, thoughts, impressions, and feelings stay with you as you meditate on this verse?

SAVOR . . .

Enjoy God's provision for your heart, soul, body, and mind. Welcome His Word with prayers of thanksgiving, confession, blessing, acknowledgment, adoration, praise, petition, and appreciation.

Where does the Holy Spirit seem to be pointing your attention as you reread and ponder this passage?

SWALLOW . . .

Receive the nourishing strength imparted to you through God's Word. Seek His wisdom, help, and understanding as His truth revives your soul.

What do you sense the Lord wants you to know, feel, or do in response to reading this passage?

DIGEST . . .

Remain with Jesus for a while longer in stillness. Rest in His presence, waiting upon His Word. Gently draw your attention back to the main passage whenever your mind wanders.

What is it you most want to say to Jesus at this moment?

Grant us help against the enemy, for deliverance by man is a vain hope. With God's help we shall do valiantly, and God himself will tread our enemies underfoot. (Ps. 108:12-13 NEB)

We find thus by experience that there is no good applying to Heaven for earthly comfort. Heaven can give heavenly comfort; no other kind. And earth cannot give earthly comfort either. There is no earthly comfort in the long run.

C. S. LEWIS

Feed on God's Word

> *Let the morning bring me word of your unfailing love, for I have put my trust in you. Show me the way I should go, for to you I lift up my soul. Rescue me from my enemies, O LORD, for I hide myself in you. Teach me to do your will, for you are my God; may your Spirit lead me on level ground. (Ps. 143:8-10)*

Taste . . .

Recognize and honor the Lord's presence as you slowly read the passage. After reading the verse two or three times, try repeating the words with your eyes closed. Direct your mind and heart toward Jesus as your thoughts dwell on His Word in silence.

What worry, concern, or burden do you need to surrender to Christ right now, so that you may more mindfully enter His presence?

Chew . . .

Listen in faith to the Lord speaking to you in His Word. Reflect upon the words in this passage with a willingness to obey God's direction, inviting Him to shape your soul's appetites and attitudes according to His design for your life.

What words, pictures, phrases, thoughts, impressions, and feelings stay with you as you meditate on this verse?

SAVOR . . .

Enjoy God's provision for your heart, soul, body, and mind. Welcome His Word with prayers of thanksgiving, confession, blessing, acknowledgment, adoration, praise, petition, and appreciation.

Where does the Holy Spirit seem to be pointing your attention as you reread and ponder this passage?

SWALLOW . . .

Receive the nourishing strength imparted to you through God's Word. Seek His wisdom, help, and understanding as His truth revives your soul.

What do you sense the Lord wants you to know, feel, or do in response to reading this passage?

DIGEST . . .

Remain with Jesus for a while longer in stillness. Rest in His presence, waiting upon His Word. Gently draw your attention back to the main passage whenever your mind wanders.

What is it you most want to say to Jesus at this moment?

Wait patiently for the LORD. Be brave and courageous. Yes, wait patiently for the LORD. (Ps. 27:14 NLT)

Oh, for the grace to be quiet! Oh, to be still and know that Jehovah is God! The holy one of Israel must defend and deliver His own. We may be sure that every word of His will stand, though the mountains should depart. He deserves to be confided in. Come, my soul, return unto thy rest, and lean thy head upon the bosom of the Lord Jesus.

ANONYMOUS, IN *STREAMS IN THE DESERT*

Feed on God's Word

Thou, LORD, my allotted portion, thou my cup, thou dost enlarge my boundaries: the lines fall for me in pleasant places, indeed I am well content with my inheritance. I will bless the LORD who has given me counsel; in the night-time wisdom comes to me in the inward parts. I have set the LORD continually before me: with him at my right hand I cannot be shaken. (Ps. 16:5-8 NEB)

Taste . . .

Recognize and honor the Lord's presence as you slowly read the passage. After reading the verse two or three times, try repeating the words with your eyes closed. Direct your mind and heart toward Jesus as your thoughts dwell on His Word in silence.

What worry, concern, or burden do you need to surrender to Christ right now, so that you may more mindfully enter His presence?

Chew . . .

Listen in faith to the Lord speaking to you in His Word. Reflect upon the words in this passage with a willingness to obey God's direction, inviting Him to shape your soul's appetites and attitudes according to His design for your life. What words, pictures, phrases, thoughts, impressions, and feelings stay with you as you meditate on this verse?

SAVOR . . .

Enjoy God's provision for your heart, soul, body, and mind. Welcome His Word with prayers of thanksgiving, confession, blessing, acknowledgment, adoration, praise, petition, and appreciation.

Where does the Holy Spirit seem to be pointing your attention as you reread and ponder this passage?

SWALLOW . . .

Receive the nourishing strength imparted to you through God's Word. Seek His wisdom, help, and understanding as His truth revives your soul.

What do you sense the Lord wants you to know, feel, or do in response to reading this passage?

DIGEST . . .

Remain with Jesus for a while longer in stillness. Rest in His presence, waiting upon His Word. Gently draw your attention back to the main passage whenever your mind wanders.

What is it you most want to say to Jesus at this moment?

The poor will eat and be satisfied; they who seek the LORD *will praise him—may your hearts live forever! (Ps. 22:26 NEB)*

True contentment is a real, even an active, virtue—not only affirmative but creative. It is the power of getting out of any situation what there is in it.

G. K. CHESTERTON

FEED ON GOD'S WORD

> *Search me, O God, and know my heart; test me and know my anxious thoughts. See if there is any offensive way in me, and lead me in the way everlasting. (Ps. 139:23-24)*

TASTE . . .

Recognize and honor the Lord's presence as you slowly read the passage. After reading the verse two or three times, try repeating the words with your eyes closed. Direct your mind and heart toward Jesus as your thoughts dwell on His Word in silence.

What worry, concern, or burden do you need to surrender to Christ right now, so that you may more mindfully enter His presence?

CHEW . . .

Listen in faith to the Lord speaking to you in His Word. Reflect upon the words in this passage with a willingness to obey God's direction, inviting Him to shape your soul's appetites and attitudes according to His design for your life.

What words, pictures, phrases, thoughts, impressions, and feelings stay with you as you meditate on this verse?

Savor . . .

Enjoy God's provision for your heart, soul, body, and mind. Welcome His Word with prayers of thanksgiving, confession, blessing, acknowledgment, adoration, praise, petition, and appreciation.

Where does the Holy Spirit seem to be pointing your attention as you reread and ponder this passage?

Swallow . . .

Receive the nourishing strength imparted to you through God's Word. Seek His wisdom, help, and understanding as His truth revives your soul.

What do you sense the Lord wants you to know, feel, or do in response to reading this passage?

Digest . . .

Remain with Jesus for a while longer in stillness. Rest in His presence, waiting upon His Word. Gently draw your attention back to the main passage whenever your mind wanders.

What is it you most want to say to Jesus at this moment?

You are my refuge and my shield; I have put my hope in your word. (Ps. 119:114)

It is love that asks, that seeks, that knocks, that finds, and that is faithful to what it finds.

ST. AUGUSTINE

Feed on God's Word

I have seen you in the sanctuary and beheld your power and your glory. Because your love is better than life, my lips will glorify you. I will praise you as long as I live, and in your name I will lift up my hands. My soul will be satisfied as with the richest of foods; with singing lips my mouth will praise you. (Ps. 63:2-5)

Taste . . .

Recognize and honor the Lord's presence as you slowly read the passage. After reading the verse two or three times, try repeating the words with your eyes closed. Direct your mind and heart toward Jesus as your thoughts dwell on His Word in silence.

What worry, concern, or burden do you need to surrender to Christ right now, so that you may more mindfully enter His presence?

Chew . . .

Listen in faith to the Lord speaking to you in His Word. Reflect upon the words in this passage with a willingness to obey God's direction, inviting Him to shape your soul's appetites and attitudes according to His design for your life.

What words, pictures, phrases, thoughts, impressions, and feelings stay with you as you meditate on this verse?

SAVOR . . .

Enjoy God's provision for your heart, soul, body, and mind. Welcome His Word with prayers of thanksgiving, confession, blessing, acknowledgment, adoration, praise, petition, and appreciation.

Where does the Holy Spirit seem to be pointing your attention as you reread and ponder this passage?

SWALLOW . . .

Receive the nourishing strength imparted to you through God's Word. Seek His wisdom, help, and understanding as His truth revives your soul.

What do you sense the Lord wants you to know, feel, or do in response to reading this passage?

DIGEST . . .

Remain with Jesus for a while longer in stillness. Rest in His presence, waiting upon His Word. Gently draw your attention back to the main passage whenever your mind wanders.

What is it you most want to say to Jesus at this moment?

I seek you with all my heart; do not let me stray from your commands. I have hidden your word in my heart that I might not sin against you. (Ps. 119:10-11)

The secret heart is devotion's temple; there the saint lights the flame of purest sacrifice, which burns unseen but not unaccepted.

HANNAH MORE